FOR THE RECKORD

FOR THE RECKORD

A COLLECTION OF THREE PLAYS
BY BARRY RECKORD

Edited by Yvonne Brewster

With contributions from Diana Athill, Pam Brighton,
Mervyn Morris and Don Warrington

OBERON BOOKS
LONDON

This collection first published in 2010 by Oberon Books Ltd
Electronic edition published in 2012

Oberon Books Ltd
521 Caledonian Road, London N7 9RH
Tel: 020 7607 3637 / Fax: 020 7607 3629
e-mail: info@oberonbooks.com
www.oberonbooks.com

Cover design by James Illman.

Cover image: Poster by Colin Garland for the Jamaica National Theatre Trust 1972 production of *In the Beautiful Caribbean* by Barry Reckord. Courtesy of Lloyd Reckord.

Visit www.oberonbooks.com to read more about all our books and to buy them. You will also find features, author interviews and news of any author events, and you can sign up for e-newsletters so that you're always first to hear about our new releases.

Dedicated to Lloyd Reckord

Contents

Prologue

In 1960, when I first met Barry Reckord, his second play, *You in Your Small Corner*, was about to open at London's Royal Court Theatre. It seems, alas, that no copy of that play survives. Being about a young Jamaican's first year in England, it was closer to his personal experience than anything else he wrote, and its run at the Court was impressive. Later it was produced again at London's Arts Theatre, but with less success owing to a bad piece of miscasting. To my mind it was the most strikingly witty of his plays.

That is the lovely quality of his writing: not the kind of wit that produces smart word-play, but wittiness in the way things are observed. Barry was never a joke-maker, but he was always acutely aware of what was absurd or comic about life, which gave his dialogue a lot of sparkle. In the same way, the elegance of his style was the kind which results in precision, rather than in a prose which is decorative or 'poetic' (something which he hated). He used to say that if you could take a word out of a sentence and substitute another one without changing the sentence's meaning, then both those words were redundant – an observation to which my own writing owes much. And this liveliness and grace of style was united with great sensitivity to moral issues, as is so powerfully demonstrated in what I think was the most admired of his plays, *Skyvers*.

It was a piece of dreadful bad luck that turned the tide of his rising reputation. *White Witch*, a marvellous play, was taken up by a producer who had enjoyed one big success in London with a play which transferred to Broadway; and Broadway was where she decided that *Witch* should open, so off Barry went to New York and glory. A director had already been picked, a cast chosen – and no sooner had they met for the first read-through than it became apparent that the producer's other play was a disastrous flop. So disastrous was it that the poor woman's career as a producer ended then and there. And Barry came home.

After that set-back, bravely though he endured it, it seemed to me that Barry's passion for ideas for their own sake began to eclipse his interest in the making of plays – and a play which exists primarily for the propagation of an idea, as his increasingly did, leaves producers cold. Gradually, therefore, the play-going public lost sight of him. But the long diminuendo with which his writing career ended most certainly ought not to annul the fact that Barry Reckord wrote four outstanding plays, and the present fact that this book brings three of them back into circulation should give great pleasure to everyone interested in serious theatre.

Diana Athill

Introduction

Why a collection of early plays from Barry Reckord? His place in the history of black playwriting in the United Kingdom goes almost unrecognised. This is unfortunate. Reckord was among the first modern Caribbean playwrights to have work produced in England, in a period when black writing was being 'discovered' there. In fact a claim might even be made that he was the first of this small band to enter the scene, if one takes into account a small fringe production of his first play *Della,* or *Adella* under which title it was staged by his brother Lloyd in London in 1954.

It was at the Royal Court Theatre in Sloane Square where the majority of Caribbean playwrights of the 1950s and 1960s found a home. In 1956 Trinidadian Errol John won *The Observer* playwriting prize with his first play *Moon on a Rainbow Shawl* which was produced there, in 1957. This was followed in 1958 by Reckord's *Flesh to a Tiger*, directed by Tony Richardson and designed by Loudon Sainthill. In 1960 *You in Your Small Corner,* written while Reckord was still a student at Cambridge, was produced by the Royal Court, directed by John Bird and produced by Michael Codron, transferring to the Arts Theatre in London's West End. It was subsequently adapted for Television by Reckord, and was aired by Granada TV on the 5th June 1962. In 1963 his third and best known play *Skyvers* was presented, once again at the Court, directed by Anne Jellicoe. These successes in the 1960s were followed in the 1970s by a stage production of a new play *A Liberated Woman¹*, Pam Brighton's updated 1971 revival of *Skyvers* which transferred from the Court to the Roundhouse, and a major BBC TV production of *In The Beautiful Caribbean²* adapted for television by Reckord, directed by Phillip Saville, leading to another BBC Television commission *Club Havana*, produced by Peter Ansorge and aired in 1975.

No scripts of Reckord's impressive body of work are readily available. They should be. My initial thought was to pull together four of the early plays. *You in Your Small Corner* would have

---

1   Presented by the Royal Court in 1971 and at La Mama in New York in March of that year.
2   First produced by The Jamaica National Theatre Trust in 1972 as a play for the stage directed by Lloyd Reckord.

been one of those but no copy has been found. The search for the texts has been challenging. Many incomplete manuscripts exist. Complete scripts were harder to come across. Finding the prompt copy of *Flesh to a Tiger* in the archives of the Royal Court held at the Victoria and Albert Museum was a eureka moment. It turned out Diana Athill had a copy of the original version of *Skyvers*, and Munair Zacca, having been persuaded to hunt in his attic of play-scripts, found *The White Witch of Rose Hall* in which he played Palmer in 1978 in Jamaica. However, during the final edit of this book Errol Lloyd unearthed a later (*White Witch* 1985) edition which had been worked on by Reckord and it is this version which is used.

Reckord's influence should be put in perspective: his achievements in England as a Jamaican abroad in the 1950s and 1960s laid a solid foundation for later emerging Caribbean playwrights such as Trinidadian Mustafa Matura, Guyanese Michael Abbensetts and Jamaican Alfred Fagon in the 1970s, all of whom appreciated how well Reckord's work had paved their way forward.

Barry Reckord described by Edward Baugh[3] as... '*an ebullient, iconoclastic prophet, willing to be reckless in his craft in order to deliver some urgent, unequivocal social message, dictated by his muse of common sense and reason...*' was, in his own words, '*...interested in sex and politics...and then in sexual politics which I didn't associate with gender. I was continually talking in my plays about sex. I agree that they were thesis driven so that when...a man walked out saying, "Me come ya fi laugh, me nuh come yah fi think," I loved that. I should've put that over my desk... My other theme was against power politics and power (sex). I usually saw them as the same syndrome... Most sex is conquest, and politics is conquest...*'[4]

In 2006 Michael Billington in his review[5] of the Royal Court 50th anniversary reading of the play wrote, '*Other dramatists such as Nigel Williams in* Class Enemy *went on to explore the failure of the system to cope with those at the bottom of the heap. But Reckord got there first and while it is tempting to say times have changed, new figures show that up to 16million adults today have the reading and writing skills of primary schoolchildren... a piece that proves the best drama offers vital social evidence.*'

---

3   Jamaican academic and man of letters.
4   *The Sunday Gleaner*, August 10 2003 section E6, Michael Reckord.
5   *The Guardian*, 25 February 2006.

So, we have three Reckord plays each written in a different decade (1950s, 1960s, 1970s) with a preface from Diana Athill, his long time friend, an introduction to *Skyvers* by Pam Brighton whom Barry says 'owns' the play by virtue of her understanding and long association with it, a detailed examination of *White Witch* by Mervyn Morris, and an appreciation of the writer as friend and mentor by the actor Don Warrington. *For the Reckord*, is hopefully, something which the growing number of new playwrights, especially but not exclusively black, will afford themselves an opportunity of reading and learning from Reckord's work or simply enjoying the sophistication and insight of his delivery, characterisation, politics and plot.

Finally, a brief introduction to *Flesh to a Tiger*... It should be understood that in the Fifties and Sixties the English Stage Company operating under the artistic leadership of George Devine at the Royal Court Theatre in Sloane Square, London was in reality the only place where new playwrights had the opportunity of having their work seriously considered, given dramaturgical advice and for the lucky few their work produced. There was no National Theatre, no Hampstead, no Soho, no Tricycle, no Talawa to approach. It was the theatre of young John Osborne whose third play *Look Back in Anger* (1956) which *'wiped the smugness off the frivolous face of English theatre*,'[6] and is credited with changing the face of modern British theatre. Thus for Jamaican Barry Reckord to have had no fewer than five of his plays, not counting in some cases second productions produced there in the face of very fierce competition from the cream of British writers such as Edward Bond, Peter Gill, John Osborne, Christopher Hampton, Anne Jellicoe and Arnold Wesker, was and remains an achievement worthy of note.

As a solitary Jamaican drama student at Rose Bruford College in 1958 vivid memories over fifty years float back to me of seeing *Flesh to a Tiger* at the Royal Court: travelling up to London to Sloane Square to see a Jamaican play was something which I had not had the opportunity of doing in London before. I had seen *Moon on a Rainbow Shawl* the previous year: that was by Trinidadian Errol John. The thought of so many Caribbean people (the performing company was over 20 strong) on a London stage was profound, but actually hearing the once

6   John Lahr, *New York Times Book Review.*

13

familiar drums, cadences and accents of my people, seeing and feeling the power of their body language, was an altogether empowering experience. The play's message for me lingers still. Bad medicine is bad medicine, be it black or white...

First presented under the title of *Della* in 1953 at Kingston's Ward Theatre it was thought to be melodramatic by some: Cynthia Wilmot (a Canadian writer and filmmaker): '*When it was good it was very, very good and when it was bad it was awful.*' Its name was changed to *Adella* for the small fringe production in London in 1954, but the 1958 title for the Royal Court production *Flesh to a Tiger* stuck.

I have found few people who actually saw *Flesh to a Tiger* in London. One such was veteran Jamaican theatre historian the late Wycliffe Bennett who happened to be in the United Kingdom at that time who recalled, '*seeing an out of town pre-premier performance in Brighton, Sussex in 1958: I remember Cleo Laine being very dynamic in this most thought producing ground breaking play*'.

The cast list read like a who's who in Black British theatre with Cleo Laine in the leading role, Nadia Cattouse, Lloyd Reckord and others. Della is an intelligent woman living in Trench Town, one of the most dis-advantaged areas of downtown Kingston. We find her estranged from the powerful local preacher cum 'natural doctor' Aaron who is mortally wounded by her defection from his church and bed...

'*I order this whole yard to shake her with silence...*'

She has two children, teenaged Joshie and ailing infant Tata who is being treated by a white doctor in open defiance of Aaron's threats to kill the infant by obeah (voodoo, black magic), his stock in trade...

'*Preacher has a thin skin and a vengeful heart,*'

is how he describes himself. Reckord's play follows Della as she is buffeted by the community's ingrained prejudice against the doctor and all he stands for, the pragmatic common sense of Joshie who sees right through the manipulative ways of the preacher and the fearful fickleness of his followers, urging his mother Della to forsake this backward approach and embrace the science which the doctor offers, and the middle class morality of the doctor who is willing to have sex with her '*...black skin graces your beauty like a fetish glove*', but not kiss her. Della is one of Reckord's most challenging parts for women. She is rarely off the stage; the emotional development of the play is dependent on her choices of action. After expelling her thoughts of succumbing to the patronising support of the doctor, she attempts to become a rallying point for the disenfranchised men and women of the area. Ultimately her hopes of leading them from the darkness of convenient if uncomfortable belief, into the light of modernity stand but a tiny chance of success thus leaving her with little option but the melodramatic.

'God's mercy fell like the bright morning over the darkness of my life...'

The play's detailed melodically written examination of the hold which religion maintains over a population which has yet to seize true emancipation from the gravity of colonisation, created tension in the auditorium and some occasional, encouraging responses from the audience who wanted her to make the right choices in her dilemma and urged her to do so:

'I hate the White Wolf (the name given the doctor by the community), *feel abomination for Shepherd. Between them, must be a way'.*

'Keep strong Della you will find a way' one urged silently, these sentiments occasionally escaping the lips, much to the annoyance of the British audience which usually prefers silent theatrical communion, echoed in the theatre.

The power of religion is an active, if at times cynical, player in the lives of many Jamaican people and has found its way into its literature, for example Alfred Fagon in *11 Josephine House,* and Perry Henzel[7] in *The Harder They Come,* who have also glanced enquiringly at the power of the men of God over their female preferably young nubile parishioners. But Barry Reckord, once again, was first.

Yvonne Brewster

---

7   Director and co-author of *The Harder They Come,* filmed in Jamaica in 1970.

FLESH TO A TIGER

Flesh to a Tiger was first Performed at the Ward Theatre Kingston, Jamaica under the title of *Della*, directed by Lloyd Reckord in 1953; the UK in 1954 in a fringe production under the title *Adella*; and then at the Royal Court in 1958 under the title *Flesh to a Tiger* with the following cast directed by Tony Richardson and designed by Loudon Sainthill:

Cast

JOSHIE, Tamba Allan

LAL, Pearl Prescod

DELLA, Cleo Laine

SHEPHERD AARON, James Clarke

THE DOCTOR, Edgar Wreford

VIE, Dorothy Blondel-Francis

GEORGE, Lloyd Reckord

PAPA G, Edmundo Otero

RUDDY, Johnny Sekka

GLORIA, Nadia Cattouse

GRANNY, Connie Smith

DRUMMERS, George Johnson, Illario Pedro, Emmanuel Myers

MEMBERS OF THE BALM YARD, Ena Babb, Maureen Seale, Lloyd Innis, Vernon Trott, Berril Briggs, Keefe West, Francisca Francis

CHILDREN, Ansel Bernard, Barbara Bernard, Auguste Curtis

Characters

JOSHIE

LAL

DELLA

SHEPHERD AARON

VIE

GEORGE

PAPA G

RUDDY

GLORIA

GRANNY

DRUMMERS

MEMBERS OF THE BALM YARD

CHILDREN

DOCTOR

Act I. Scene   1. Afternoon.
2. Night.
3. Next morning.
4. Late afternoon.

Act II. Scene 1. Early evening.
2. do.
3. do.
4. Night.
5. do.
6. do.
7. do.

Act One

SCENE ONE

JOSHIE is sitting on a log in the yard. DELLA is in the house sitting on a stool facing upstage, nursing the baby, singing a lullaby.

Enter LAL.

LAL: Joshie! True what they say Joshie?

JOSHIE: Who say, Miss Lal?

LAL: What they say about Tata.

JOSHIE: Who say?

Drum.

LAL: Shepherd Aaron.

JOSHIE: Shepherd Aaron work obeah on my brother to kill him, then spread it around he soon dead. Miss Lal, you didn't hear doctor say obeah is just silly black magic?

LAL: Obeah silly black magic. What more say the doctor?

JOSHIE: Doctor say give him a little time Tata soon better.

LAL: Joshie, Shepherd Aaron say that doctor is a hell doctor; more, he is a white man. I feel for Tata as my own child, but I know who have the healing power.

JOSHIE: One whole year Shepherd Aaron work on the baby, while my mother was living with him. You were with us then. And Shepherd could find no cure for Tata.

LAL: The doctor find cure?

JOSHIE: In one month?

LAL: More than a month.

JOSHIE: Give him time.

LAL: The Shepherd Aaron is a terrible man. You see how Tata wither up, wither up dying from fever. That same doctor said Vie called him too late, but Shepherd Aaron laugh. Your mother inside?

JOSHIE: With Tata.

LAL: I want to help, to show my sympathy.

She begins walking away. JOSHIE calls her back.

JOSHIE: Miss Lal.

LAL: Joshie?

JOSHIE: My mother confidence the doctor. Don't frighten her.

Miss LAL raps tentatively on DELLA's door. She calls softly.

LAL: Adella.

DELLA: Oh, Lal, I glad you come. I hear the voice talking to Joshie and strain my ears but couldn't make out it was you. You talk so soft.

LAL: Soon now I will bawl my throat out and Tata's ears won't catch a word. *(Full of pity she looks at TATA.)* How God punish you for that day you leave the Shepherd.

DELLA: How many times my conscience walked out his house but my feet couldn't follow it. But when that girl Liza left Shepherd's flock, and to take vengeance he turned on her, filled her ears with whispers of crippling and death, so gradually she fall off her play and her food, her mind turn wild, her flesh hot, and in agony she dead; then God's mercy fell like the bright morning over the darkness of my life with Shepherd, and with my own baby so long sick, inveigled me to run to a doctor with him. Run, Lal. A power drove me greater than Shepherd and my feet couldn't stand firm against the stream of it.

LAL: Not power. You love the white man. It excite you to find a white man will mix with you.

DELLA: I risk my baby life to get a white man?

LAL: Yes. Doctor sweet as breeze. Not a day pass but he down here seeing Tata. Yet Tata is still... *(She searches for a word and finally uses a euphemism that at the same time suggests what a change the sickness has brought about on the child she helped to nurse.)* not himself. *(Almost screams.)* Why doctor don't take the child to hospital?

DELLA: He was waiting for a bed.

LAL: All this time?

DELLA: They lie three to a cot in the hospital. You won't catch my child there.

LAL: The bed doctor want is down here. He know too many of us living to bother with the sick, so he venture Tata for a spree with the black gal.

DELLA: Lie, lie, lie. He is a gentleman to me. Joshie love him. Savagery drive me from Shepherd and the doctor's gentlemanliness keep me. How Shepherd moved through his women with no reverent feeling, mashed them in his mouth like ripe bananas to fill a maw that soon emptied out again. Any tenderness he dropped was only seed to lure me to a dry spring. His eye pitched on no beauty he wouldn't swallow, flesh and bone and feather. I tell you, Lal, I thought once what made me leave Shepherd was a sudden mood. But it was a deep instinct surging strong from the bottom of me. I hate his power, solid as the earth, and pray I could gather up strength like an earthquake and shake him.

LAL: While you stay here fretting yourself, Shepherd easy. Like a god he order his people, they cut you off. You starve and Joshie and Tata, while he don't feel the crumb of hunger.

DELLA: If only I could get a chance to leave Trench Town. I believe, I believe doctor and me fit so like hat and head, that before long he will ask me to come work with him in St. Andrew.

LAL: Among all the white people?

DELLA: I tell you Lal, the lowest servant work would content me. Every morning I pray to God, "temper Doctor's heart and make him want me to come, and make him ask me"; for me this Trench Town dark, with limber devils in it.

LAL: You put it to him already?

DELLA: Sometime now. I suggest; get no notice. Then again I hint, go round, come round, hint again.

LAL: M-m-m. And he not out with anything yet.

DELLA: He looked at me from under his eye. Don't rightly know how to take it, but he is so perfect I think there's a hope one day he will say to me, "Della come."

LAL: *(Laughs.)* You know he live by himself.

DELLA: He not low down like Shepherd you know. I don't think women trouble him at all. But if he has me, he has me. And I tell you Lal, I'd be glad, for a sick baby can't fill a woman's ache.

LAL: And white man won't fill it neither. You believe when you keep house for him he would take you decently and give you joy. In their Bible it says wolf and lamb lie down together. But they never mix up religion and business. No, you're black, and white man would scorn you.

DELLA: I'm not expecting him to touch me; but it wouldn't be that he scorn me; that doctor could desire to caress me like a night wind but is too high a man to take the pleasure he is not married to.

Drum.

LAL: Caress you. No Della. The sympathy that would caress, long time now would invite you to a decent living. The Doctor fear if he touch you at all it would be to swell up

and sweep over you. That man would batter you like a
hurricane; flash his lightning against you, and walk 'way
leave you. For black to white is flesh to a tiger. When they
come 'cross it, they tear it.

DELLA: Say no more.

LAL: But he's a timid man. All this storminess frighten him so
he dare not touch you.

They stop speaking and we hear JOSHIE's pipe.

DELLA: I begged Joshie not to play that tune. Makes my blood
run cold.

LAL: I must go now, Adella.

DELLA: No, no you can't do that. I'm so glad you come. At
night I sit alone, and hear the boy groan and catch up
his breath. Lord, Miss Lal, I wish I wasn't alone. Why
everybody keep so far from the sick Miss Lal? No answer.
But you know why. You know the whole street tremble
under Shepherd Aaron rod. But I tell the world Shepherd
can't harm me or mine if I lie down like a lamb in Jesus
Christ. *(Calls out.)* Joshie, I beg you stop playing that tune.
(To LAL.) It reminds me too much of the Shepherd. *(Tune
stops.)* Your belly empty out and you don't feel safe outside
him… You know I leave Shepherd now nigh two month
and is the first time you come to see me. God knows I
would do well to fear the Shepherd because he turn every
eye from me, every mind he turn from me, and only Joshie
and Tata know when I cry.

*Faintly begins to be heard a sound of drums and singing. It is a march
of SHEPHERD and his balm-yard and they seem to be coming in the
direction of DELLA's house.*

LAL: You hear it, Della, you hear it? Shepherd danger song.

JOSHIE calls from outside.

JOSHIE: Me mother, you hear the music?

DELLA: Call in Joshie, Lal.

JOSHIE has already come rushing in.

JOSHIE: I ran down the road and saw Shepherd, boasty, wheeling his staff like a regimental sergeant-major. Every five minutes he wheeled round and curled up and bowed to the young ladies in the procession. Run out and see his red cloak and Jordan banner, and how he breathe hard and shake his head and snuffle his nose like the ram-goat at Government stud-farm.

DELLA: The sound draw nearer.

JOSHIE: You might be able to stay here and see them. I see that lady Vie, an' she dress up like red-stick spinach in seed. You should see her. She was a bowing fool. The sun hot and the dust thick, but she was in the spirit.

DELLA: The sound draw nearer.

LAL: They're singing. "Death Oh my Lord". Is the Shepherd danger song. Vie turned away from Shepherd but she come back. Adella, to turn is a fearful thing. I won't stay in this house any longer. Go back to Shepherd. He slay Vie's daughter Liza, he have the power.

Exit LAL.

DELLA: *(Weeping.)* Joshie, he coming this way. Lal tear up my courage like old newspaper. If he come now...

JOSHIE: Mama!

DELLA: Stay with me, Joshie.

JOSHIE: You can't stand up to him, but I going to call the doctor. Let me go quick. If is this yard he coming to, he might block up my way.

DELLA: I weak, I can't stand up...

JOSHIE: The doctor will drive him away. I'll bring back the doctor.

JOSHIE is cut off by the SHEPHERD and his followers who are by now in the foreground dancing and harmonising. At the end SHEPHERD cries.

SHEPHERD: Amen. Hold up your banner high. Wipe off the sweat streaming down like Christ's blood. The Good Shepherd will rescue his sheep from the doctor White-Wolf. Sing it out.

His followers break into a perfectly harmonised wail of the hymn 'There were ninety and nine that safely lay, in the shelter of the fold.' JOSHIE makes a dash at passing, but SHEPHERD intercepts.

Joshie, boy.

JOSHIE: I got nutten to say to you. I know who will answer you.

SHEPHERD: You, an upright boy, black like me, take umbrage 'gainst me. I surprise Joshie. What gives boy?

JOSHIE: Give me pass.

WOMAN IN THE CROWD: Boy, have respect. Where you want pass to go to?

JOSHIE: Ruffians, give me pass.

SHEPHERD: Ruffian? That is White-Wolf word. He howl it out. Never let it echo from your mouth. Where your mother?

JOSHIE: *(Mockingly shielding his eyes and peering into the crowd.)* Look like she not with you, Shepherd.

SHEPHERD: Boy, the sun hot, the dust high, me temper short. Tell your mother Shepherd call her. Tell her to bring Tata out and make her peace with me. *(To his followers.)* Hum the peace song, sing it out. Make it touch Della's heart.

SHEPHERD leads off "AMEN"; all join in humming. DOCTOR appears.

JOSHIE: Me mother, doctor come.

DOCTOR: Give Tata poison, Aaron, and you can harm him. But your hymns can't hurt him and your magic can't help him.

Humming stops.

SHEPHERD: Black God. Black Christ, come judge between man and monster, make the monster leave off Adella's bed, Adella's body.

The CHORUS groans.

DOCTOR: Adella's bed be damned. When I start practising to come by a bed I'll be as insatiable a cock as you.

SHEPHERD: Sing it out. She lie down with the White-Wolf, but come the black lion, fear take the suckling; it whimper, she clutch it, but surely it dead. What is the word?

CHORUS: Death.

DELLA screams. SHEPHERD and his followers exit with a low, breathless chant, SHEPHERD having made his obeah mark on the ground.

DELLA: Is the same way they call when Vie daughter dead. And now Tata will sink lower into that vale. God strike off this charm from my baby that Shepherd set; I can't tear it off.

DOCTOR: *(Intones.)* Tata's all right. There's no charm on your baby. Calm Della, Shepherd has no power. Rest. There's no charm.

DELLA: *(Hysterically.)* He have his hand round Tata throat. Feel the jaws tight. Oh, my belly heavy.

DOCTOR: Calm now, quietly. You won't be frightened by two silly marks on the ground.

DELLA: He kill their children, rob their money; crawl over the whole body of them like dog flea. Balm-yard people are dogs and Shepherd suck their blood. Doctor, you are

a friend brushing stinging wasps from me, brushing away
spiders that grip, grip, grip at my heart.

DOCTOR: We want the whole balm-yard away from Shepherd.
It's not only the jumping at the meetings, wearing
themselves out night after night. It's the brutal stupidity
and flourish of ignorance.

DELLA: Joshie, go fetch Tata water.

DOCTOR: Rest Della.

DELLA: Doctor, you have space for a servant at your yard?

DOCTOR: I'm a doctor, not an employer.

DELLA: A servant couldn't come nowhere near your privacy.
She live in an outhouse.

DOCTOR: If she stayed in the outhouse. But rest. When I say
rest, rest. You're not a child. Close your eyes. Breathe deep.
Lord, woman, you're your own terror, killing yourself.

DELLA: I not excited any more.

DOCTOR: Well, after a month with me, frightened at the first
puff of Shepherd.

DELLA: I try to remedy this fear of obeah, but it cover me like
flesh. When I die I'll be rid of it. But a healthy roof for me
and my children would help cure it.

DOCTOR: A bachelor's servant must be a shrivelled up old
cow so the neighbours won't whisper.

DELLA: Is a slim chance they would whisper. But you would
let me starve rather than take it.

DOCTOR: A young Queen of Sheba needn't beg. Any day,
today, five men would vie for you.

DELLA: Like five dogs for a bitch. Doctor, this place unsettle
my mind; I'm not well. I need a friend to take me out of it.

DOCTOR: I suppose I should go ahead and take you. I
suppose. All my life I've supposed and left it at that.
Coming down here was the only thought I've ever acted
out. Acted out!! Jesus. Isn't that just what it is.

DELLA: You ever frightened yet, Doctor, 'bout your food
supply? When I was with Shepherd he get in clothes
for me to wash. Now I still get in a trickle, but I watch it
dwindle. I watch them squeeze me out.

DOCTOR: You rake up the coals, eh Della. For a long time the
misery down here rested on my mind. So to ease my ache
I dreamed. It preserved my sleep. But I did wake up and
came down here.

DELLA: If you're not giving me relief from Trench Town, is
better Tata dead. For without him I could wander, and seek
work, and make myself again, even on the wages pittance.

DOCTOR: Don't chide me, Della. I've done something – I'm
not God. Doesn't your Bible say each must bear his own
burden?

DELLA: Also, bear each other's burdens.

DOCTOR: Yes, mutual frustrations often have a common
solution. Heaven knows I do my share for you and the
devil couldn't trap me into more. Here's a pound Della.
I must run before the fire in my belly starts to burn me,
stronger than the outside sun.

Exit the DOCTOR.

*DELLA tears the pound and throws it down on the ground. JOSHIE
rushes to pick it up.*

JOSHIE: He give you a pound and you tear it up. Why you
vexed? You should be glad. Is the first time Doctor give us
money. I going to paste it.

DELLA: If you see a stray dog hungry on the street, what use to
throw bread to it? After you're gone it range hungry again.
Sympathy would take it home and care it, or send it to the

police to put out its life. Then if you wouldn't throw scraps to a dog, you shouldn't throw them neither to a woman, her boy and baby. *(In desperation.)* He can't leave me here in Trench Town to Shepherd torment.

JOSHIE: We could leave.

DELLA: If I was alone I could perhaps get a job. But who going to employ me with Tata.

JOSHIE: Someone might take pity.

DELLA: Pity? Must I wait on pity? Sooner than walk out of Trench Town and wander and beg, as God live and as vengeance against Him, I would go back to Shepherd and degrade myself in the yard, mingling with every man, and whore on the street.

JOSHIE: Tomorrow, make one more try.

DELLA: Tomorrow I will beg him again. Tonight pray he won't harden his heart without cause 'gainst my need.

SCENE TWO

SHEPHERD's room. He is going through obeah ritual, lighting a candle, blowing on the flame, until it flutters, then blowing it out. He does this several times, with great earnestness.

SHEPHERD: Little wick, feeling the death wind, go mad with terror, then out. Out with Tata *(He calls someone offstage.)* Frank, run next door and call Lal to me. This morning I took the word death to Tata. Yet a baby can't catch the word, and hold it to his heart, flutter like this flame, then out. If Tata didn't hear the word, he can't conceive the fear, nor Della whisper to him her own fright. And without the word all the hundred elements of obeah at work come to nothing.

A knocking. LAL enters.

Lal, you visit Della this morning.

LAL: Yes, Shepherd, I visit Della but…

SHEPHERD: But you false, since I lay stringent command on the whole yard to shake her with silence.

LAL: I only breeze in and breeze out again to warn her your power high. It wasn't as a friend I went to her but as an omen.

SHEPHERD: Silence was my omen and through it Della would've felt Shepherd's hand reaching up on her, gently, to take her away.

LAL: I sure she feel your hand.

SHEPHERD: I never asked you assure nutten. I gave you a command to obey. What you say, Lal?

LAL: I beg your pardon?

SHEPHERD: Think whether pardon can brew again that silence your busy-ness spill over. How the beat of the danger music this morning would melt her heart, if for three weeks, tormented, and straining her ears in a silent desert for news of the Shepherd, this was the first sound.

LAL: Shepherd, Shepherd, I went to her room out of sympathy for her. I can't help sympathy. I don't know what to do.

SHEPHERD: Perhaps you can make up for the wrong you did. Tata is a baby and his mind doesn't yet move on the voice of the Shepherd. The magic I sprinkle on him from a distance touch him, sicken him already as you know. But rightful obeah need not only magic but the word and how a baby to hear it? So if Tata hang on to life, you must release him.

LAL looks up in terror.

You visit Della once, visit her again; turn the baby over on his belly, press his nose down on the pillow. Who will miss him? Della won't miss him. She will rejoice death come take him.

LAL: Murder, Shepherd? God's messenger murder? I leaving this room.

She starts to walk out.

SHEPHERD: Mind your two feet betray you, you crawl out. If I leave my mark on you, you tremble before you age.

LAL weeps helplessly.

You would set a baby, every night they bury one in the Trench Town heap – set a shrivelled-up baby before my need. Fearful Lal, answer Della's question whether I have power even over death, and she will come back to do the name of Shepherd reverence with all the balm-yard.

LAL: You grasping. More people in your balm-yard than eggs in a fly's belly, yet this one woman you can't leave alone. Well, forget your name and leave her and her child.

SHEPHERD: Shepherd has a thin skin and a vengeful heart.

LAL: Are you God, that if one soul leave you, your palms itch?

SHEPHERD: All, is the peace of Shepherd's soul.

LAL: Della…

SHEPHERD: Swallow that name. Know that she wrong me. This morning she held me to a grindstone and doctor turned. The whole yard watch him grind me and I fight him, all the same to them if I lose, ready to fall away one by one to him.

LAL: True, Shepherd. So black man fickle.

SHEPHERD: And she, that for white-man love stir up all this, I'll slow burn with fire and brimstone. Tata is only a start. I goin' shake her. I goin' shut down my teeth on her.

LAL: Calm yourself. What Della stir up, Tata will settle, and behind the name of Shepherd is a full breeze.

SHEPHERD: Though the yard full you should know my reputation dwindling in my age. And I too old now to join the strong young men hardening their arse on the side-walks of Kingston, finding out bread not easy to beg. Those doctors can't do more than us, but they're out to mash up all obeah men's business to improve their own. They do mind cure, so do we, and better them because we do it from a distance. They use chemistry, we use herbs; and plenty who spend out money on them get cured by us. Now into his hand who is less than the equal of me Della put power of me? God...

LAL: I will visit Della and try to put a staff of fear round her neck and lead her back.

SHEPHERD: So I can plead with her to murder her own baby?

LAL: Not for God 'self will I break the commandment.

SHEPHERD: Lord, if now when I have a grip on White-Wolf windpipe Lal won't strengthen me, I must clip it with my own hand.

LAL: Shepherd, already Tata bad sick and the magic will suffice. Bide your fear. Wait one day, two days. God will let him out.

SHEPHERD: You know he sick bad?

LAL: A month and he not recovered yet. He will pass over.

SHEPHERD: What if in two days he not dead?

LAL: Never mind. Never try to span God's purpose. Two days long.

Exit LAL.

SHEPHERD: Little wick feeling the death wind go mad with terror, then out. Out with Tata.

SCENE THREE

DELLA: Even his eyes puffy. The shadow of Shepherd passing over him. I go 'gainst experience when I take him to doctor. I pray I won't rue it.

JOSHIE: You've left Shepherd once and for good; you have no more to do with him. Now you're with doctor and he will heal Tata. Mama, what really worry you?

DELLA: Tata's everlasting sickness. And I have to beg to get servant work. If I work as servant, as servant you will work. And God knows I so chafe under the wicked chance that order who is servant and who is boss that often I feel I would grapple with it. Oh, Joshie, why my mind always drag me to questions that burn inside me? Boss me, and I hush them up, hush them up.

JOSHIE: See him coming now. I going out the back way.

DELLA: Why?

JOSHIE: I too anxious to see him.

Exit JOSHIE as DOCTOR enters.

DOCTOR: I saw a shadow move across the room. Was it Joshie's? Did he want us to be alone.

DELLA: He couldn't stay, Doctor. He's over anxious.

DOCTOR: Could he get work, Della?

DELLA: He had a metal trade and stuck to it, but I found them misusing him and took him away. A number of young men these quarters have no labour to hand.

DOCTOR: And find women to support them… I suppose that if Tata could get into hospital you would find work more easily.

DELLA: And after he get better, Doctor?

DOCTOR: Sufficient unto the day.

DELLA: You don't think he will get better?

DOCTOR: He'll get well again… How many young men have you supported in your time?

DELLA: I was married, sir.

DOCTOR: No offence, Dell. Your husband carved out for himself the warm heart of the world and left it cold.

DELLA: Doctor, I going to have let part of this room. The gentleman I letting it to say he will pass a screen down the middle.

DOCTOR: Gentleman! The gentleman has an eye for a bargain.

DELLA: I have no choice.

DOCTOR: But to live in a crevice with a sweaty brute of a lecher planning to move in on you from the other side. I can just see the grease under his broken nail, the food hiding in his cavities sucked out with relish between advances from the screen to the bed. God, to think that ultimately you'd stomach that flesh pot.

DELLA: You leave me no choice.

DOCTOR: I wouldn't have you a truckler bed for anything.

DELLA: You only know the shame of the stab I get in my useless front. But the shame all Negroes suffer, the shame of the kick Joshie get in his pants you don't know. Once your sort of shame filled me, but now it dry up to a trickle. If only I could get the clothes to wash or the bed to make, I should do my day's work and be content to lie in my outroom bed like a dog, and sleep.

DOCTOR: And when you fall to heat, stray down to Trench Town again? Are you dead to feeling for your own loveliness? The black skin graces your beauty like a fetish glove, draws me to your glove like a fitting hand.

DELLA: I'm old shoes; who ever polish, wear.

DOCTOR: Can you feel the breeze cooling the sun on your face?

DELLA: In your sleep this morning an angel must have brushed a feather over your tongue.

DOCTOR: *(Resting his hand on her shoulder.)* I want to see your eyes announcing that smile. Be happier now. Don't go back to thinking of Tata and this room.

DELLA: I feel you are the boy grew up with me in the country; we used to spend the whole day together, and wade in the river, my dress rolled into my pants. One day I kissed him and he kissed me and kissed me again till I pushed him into the water. Don't leave me longer to the bitterness of this room.

DOCTOR: You're never here but live in my mind a possession, unpossessed. Your body like dark supple water draws my thirst. Now your side rests in my hand, I touch your breast, I draw you round me like a garment for my strength.

DELLA: Come to my lips.

DOCTOR: They don't compel me.

DELLA: You scorn me.

DOCTOR: When I hold you like this?

DELLA: You must come to my lips. A man will risk his privy, but scorn lies in the lips.

DOCTOR: Too many mouths have drooled over them.

She kisses him, he hurls her away.

Why didn't you ask for money instead of my lips? I won't kiss three in a bed.

DELLA is lost. She tries to speak and says nothing. The DOCTOR adjusts his clothing and collects his bag.

Never mind, it's not your fault, I started it. Goodbye.

Exit DOCTOR. DELLA breaks down in sobs.
In a few minutes LAL enters.

LAL: Della, ease your heart; don't draw your curtain 'gainst me. You shouldn't make a white scornmonger break you down.

DELLA: Little while he open himself out to me, called me
pretty colour words, draw me out of my temper, 'til
my love hang on to him and hug him and talk out as it
feel. Oh, Lal, when the man lash me, a slave hide come
over my flesh, and back to a slave heart my free heart
dwindle, dwindle without a twinge, like it was born to that
space. But from that slavery I will haul it out, feed it with
vengeance. I swear an oath, Lal. Though starvation shrink
my belly till it dry with hunger, though Tata die, though
Shepherd Aaron power lash me till I bleed pain, though
his darkness enclose me till my eyes fix open and I can't
vent a cry, I vomit all white flesh and cover it with dust.

LAL: Yes. You let wishing confuse you. Nothing in this world
better than the safety of the yard. Go back to Shepherd.

DELLA: I hate White Wolf and feel abomination for Shepherd.
Between them must lie a way.

LAL: Which way, my love? Shepherd is your own people.

DELLA: Your own people don't have a savage heart, bitter gut
and craving belly?

LAL: But they don't turn down one eye and make up their
voice and kindly animalise you… When you complain all
your beauty pleads before my pity. Think the man done
nothing for Tata and yet… but dry your eye now, Miss
Della, blow your nose. I wish I could lend you a kerchief to
snuffle your heart.

DELLA: *(She laughs the way one does after crying.)* Your kindness
reach further than kerchief.

LAL: And I will never take it back.

JOSHIE enters.

JOSHIE: Hi, Miss Lal. *(Going to DELLA.)* Doctor agrees to it?

DELLA: No.

JOSHIE: He gives reason?

DELLA: He has reason.

JOSHIE: He says anything about Tata?

DELLA: He will take him to hospital.

LAL: It late, for now Tata too poorly.

JOSHIE: Take off your mouth.

DELLA: Joshie!

JOSHIE: How can you sit there not near the boy and feel that he poorly? Don't bother believe yourself a Shepherd.

LAL: I will go and take my feelings with me.

She kisses TATA.

DELLA: Joshie, you're so in love with white man you hurt your own?

JOSHIE: Tata not going die.

LAL: This pale shade look to me like death.

JOSHIE: Is only fever pale.

LAL: What you know?

JOSHIE: If I was an old woman you would believe me.

LAL: Old woman sage.

JOSHIE hurries away from the bedside, covers his head with a rag like an old woman, humps his back and shuffles back to the bed.

JOSHIE: Fever pale. No cause to fret, Lal; you young yet; fever pale.

DELLA: Joshie.

LAL: Jesus, boy, don't crack jokes at your brother's death. Look at the blood come down into the baby's eye, Della. Call Shepherd, the baby's dying.

JOSHIE: Doctor says we must call him the slightest thing happen to Tata.

DELLA: Call nothing. He got no more right in this house.

JOSHIE however dashes past her.

Come with me to the hospital, Lal.

LAL: Let me go call Shepherd. When God crown the King you must obey him though he harder than all troubles. Shepherd is King.

DELLA: Leave me then Lal.

LAL: All right. I will come with you to the hospital.

During the last few lines a crowd has gathered outside DELLA's house. As DELLA and LAL come out they are met with hostile looks. DELLA slowly, proudly moves through them. The crowd move slowly after her. LAL exits hurriedly ahead of DELLA, the crowd begin to sing derisively, quietly, then gaining in volume "Gal, your drawers are dropped." As DELLA reaches the exit, downstage-left GEORGE enters, and as DELLA exits he crosses angrily to PAPA G. who, heading the crowd, has now reached centre.

GEORGE: *(Seizing PAPA G. which silences the singing.)* Her baby's dying.

KEEFE: Well, she soon raise up another one.

CROWD laugh.

FRANCESCA: This time from the white man.

CROWD laugh, then pick up the song again and leave GEORGE and VERNON standing centre as they exeunt generally.

GEORGE: Some people is a bitch!

The lights fade.

SCENE FOUR

Late afternoon. The scene opens several hours later with LAL talking to the DOCTOR in DELLA's room.

LAL: No, sit down there and wait; whole evening we were at that hopsital, and no attention. But the baby eye was clearing up so Della's had a little ease. Then the blood came down into the eyes again, and Della get up and run with the baby to a nurse who say she would quickly put her in to see the doctor; but it was another wait, wait, wait, everlasting while madness mount up in Della and she choke with her grief. Doctor, no attention for a child this whole God Almighty day.

DOCTOR: Why didn't she ask for me? *(Slipping into superiority.)* If he isn't seen to he will naturally die.

LAL: *(Meekly.)* I say that to her. She say "Suppose she didn't know you, the child wouldn't have attention?" She well stubborn. She should ask for you even so that you could take her in to see another man.

DOCTOR: She wanted another man, did she?

LAL: She feel that now you not seeing her you wouldn't want to bother with her son.

DOCTOR: Where is she?

LAL: Gone next door to try and borrow money.

DOCTOR: For a private doctor? Does she leave Tata here alone so the whole of Trench Town can doctor him?

LAL: Not a soul will touch him, doctor. From Tata born I help her look after him.

DOCTOR: All the same, I wish *she* never left him.

LAL: Only seldom she leave him.

DOCTOR: Never is what I wanted. Never. That blasted Shepherd would creep through a crevice.

LAL: I'm as anxious for Tata as you! I nursed this child. When, as the sickness begun, he was devilish all night, I was gentle with him. I brought him to life again.

Very hurt, LAL exits.
Enter DELLA.

DELLA: The time come now when the bramble I grab to save myself root up, and the sharp hill slope ready to bruise my body the way down, till it hit bottom, dead. All happen as Shepherd will. First Liza, now Tata.

DOCTOR: Tata will live. You know it. You talk for revenge.

DELLA: Revenge, Doctor? You're too high for me to revenge myself on.

DOCTOR: If you use sarcasm, Della, I'll leave this room this instant.

DELLA: I wish you never come. It not a room you come to but a whore-house.

DOCTOR: Believe now it has become a room again, and we share so completely the same flesh that I can feel your body's anger in mine.

DELLA: I believe you. All this month the hints for you to take me for scrubbing your floor; you pass me over. I swallow my shame and hint again, you throw me a piece of money to dry up the detestable mouth water dropping round you. Why now this worry about me?

DOCTOR: Well then, come, come and work. I beg you now. Come and work with me.

DELLA: How you bright with courage. But it will travel over like this day's sun and come to cold darkness. Yet even if it did shine, you think my life should lay on your tongue? Lord Jesus, if you can see Della's mind now lean, even leap to the desire to servant this gentleman, then he is justified for so soon as he whistle the poor bitch he lame with a kick, wag her tail and whine.

DOCTOR: In place of that kick which made me more barbarous than snarls and fangs and brutishness, I offer a kiss. *(He kisses her hard, unresponsive cheek.)*

DELLA: When I walk the street just now after the murder you did my love, and saw my people, every one of them a nasty poorhouse with a sweat smell, a vision come to me, my mind feed on it. You come to Africa, cut me off from the people that know me, the hut my own hand thatch. You drag me, whip me, cover distance with me. Into a ship you pitch me and squeeze me down with a hundred more black people you tear from their ground limb from joint; they bawl and scream out, some stave in their skulls on the ship wood. When I cast my eye back, nothing I know fill it but salt water. Over all the living creep weakness and fear and silence. Sea salt and fire from the bare sun, and in the dungeon you leave us in, no air. Heat settle over our flesh like strait-jacket. Every day they drown the mad, clear the dead and fatten the living: bed the women for their lust and the life that would grow wild in them, the mulatto baby branded in the womb. When my people rich like you, when good health and smart dress bring out their beauty, offer your kiss, for then, like the kiss of air and earth it will have foundation.

DOCTOR: You will go back to the Shepherd. Once bitten, twice bitten.

DELLA: Someone going to bring to this Trench Town a destiny. And if is Della, that destiny will be neither Shepherd's obeah, nor the unnatural scorn of White Wolf.

DOCTOR: Couldn't we get back to working hard together over Tata? You were getting on then.

DELLA: You taught me to air the room and let light in through the window.

DOCTOR: And Tata didn't die, Tata lived.

DELLA: Light and air can't give life; but only the spirit can spy out slavery and rifle it.

DOCTOR: You're certain?

DELLA: I certain.

DOCTOR: Goodbye, Della.

He exits.

DELLA: Goodbye Doctor. *(To JOSHIE.)* Brace up your sorrow. Don't think your mother light. The white man didn't do justice by me.

JOSHIE: I wish I was another woman son.

DELLA: Don't hold anger 'gainst me.

JOSHIE: Remember how he gentle.

DELLA: In himself he gentle, and among his own colour. But Joshie, if a man look down on you as earth and treasure himself as air how can gentleness change the elements? Earth must be black and air must be sweet till death. So, content yourself, my dear boy, with me and Lal and Shepherd. We have the same soil and the same worm.

JOSHIE: With Shepherd. You going back to Shepherd?

DELLA: I must pray him help our people span the bitter breach between black and white.

JOSHIE: Pray Aaron? A money fly like him?

DELLA: The people are his sheep. The ways with sheep are a mystery to me, but well known to Shepherd.

JOSHIE: Mama, we must graft ourselves on to white people, for what we want they got – houses and fruitful land. We have candle and brushwood; they have science and make good light. They have history and learning. They had the strength to beat us up and bring us to this land.

DELLA: White worm has bored into you and will eat you out.

JOSHIE: All I know is that our people ugly, nasty, ignorant and smell.

DELLA: Then they smell of the filth white people pitch on
    them and are nasty because they haven't yet found out
    the path to that high spring will wash it off. Who will lead
    them to that high spring? Not my own son, for he out to
    shove his hefty foot into white man boot and don't know
    yet it will squeeze him. You want to make a marriage
    between black and white. The run of such marriage is not
    between flesh and flesh but between whip and back. So
    make sure when you hand them a wife, they don't fancy
    her a whore.

ACT TWO

SCENE ONE

Early Evening. SHEPHERD in his room, tipsy, drinking rum and crackers. A series of raps on the door.

SHEPHERD: Say first if you have black skin for White Wolf would give me such a bite in my belly, but on black skin his teeth break. *(Knock.)* Come in if you have black skin, for now if he black, I would welcome my enemy... But black Della conspired with white man to fall Shepherd.. *(Knock.)* If you black, keep out... Fool to buy crackers with weevil... black people grow weevils in their guts. White makes them a smooth tomb.

Knock. A voice muffled by the rain calls out.

Shove the door.

Enter DELLA.

Ho, ho, ho, a stubborn bitch like you, soon as your baby starts his journey to the grave, comes running back? Your Doctor patched and patched but still the life leak out, till now Tata sag. I so drunk I can't lay hand on you to crunch you like crackers, go out black and white whore. Your skin black, but your mouth must be white from playing with the white man.

DELLA: *(She kneels.)* On my knee, Shepherd, I never have nutten to do with him.

SHEPHERD: I guess not on your knee, but on your belly you play with him. Go out. I say go out. Your ears not so black they can't hear.

DELLA: Your eyes not so red they can't see. I come on my knee to explain, to beg.

SHEPHERD: On your knee, yes, on your knee before the power of God's people.

DELLA: You know your power over Liza drive me 'way.

SHEPHERD: And my power over Tata bring you back.

DELLA: Your colour, your blood, your kinship bring me back. Use the power Tata put in your hand to help Tata people. Let them feel the white man spread out lies over them, to coop them up and keep them down. Make them rip open, steal out into the wide space and sense the cramp of the cell. Oh, Shepherd, our people have a live mind, but the habit of reverence for the white man chain it, and though it bark, it can't spring.

SHEPHERD: I've got no more to fear from White-Wolf than from negro. All who come to the yard know two or three old herb women they believe in their heart are deadlier than me. They believe in old women; and all of them, even some of the children, believe in themselves. See them when the full moon come tie their heads with red cloth, see them in the early morning draw herbs. Or they believe in rings, or put Bible over water and read a dreadful psalm. Policemen are just dying to see me stumble because they tall like me, and carry guns and work for the Queen, yet don't possess my name and authority. But the joke is, Lord God, it's sweet, they afraid to arrest me. Most of them were born right in Trench Town here, where people have respect.

DELLA: Respect for what, Shepherd? Respect for spirits? That's what you teaching them: fear the spirits, fear this house, fear that neighbour, fear the evil eye; from the spirits come bad luck and sickness?

SHEPHERD: Yes. When I command them. Watch Tata.

DELLA: So I must come to Shepherd and sing 'way the spirits and make them wither under his prayer, and under his wonderful hand? Father, you were a carpenter once. When we come to the yard, tell us about the work and money and skill we need to be even with any man. With all these people round you this town should be a fortress with our flag flying high and fighting men in it. Not blind bodies feeling after spirits. No wonder they straying from you.

SHEPHERD: So I will lash them to me with the obeah whip. Today I stroll down the street, the children stub them nose 'gainst the window-pane and wonder to see Shepherd. The mother sigh, the father shame to know he must cower under obeah. Obeah is the strength of the yard, to hook your neck, Della, when you stray, and to exalt Shepherd.

DELLA: Exalt you. But what about your people? When the Government pitch tins of rejected milk on the damp foul-brown dungheap next door to us, some of your women run to the dump, half-laughing with shame, their old slippers dragging along the pavement. The old milk truck rest on the dump and young and old attack it, screaming, tugging, rooting among the refuse, driving off the swine. Your women, once they lose their shame, are the best rooters, using their weight and demureness to trample on the little boys and fill their own pans with the rancid milk. When, last year, that place had just become the dump, some of these same women loudly called out 'gainst this grubbing for garbage. It was 'gainst dignity. But time and need for us have worn out dignity. Their little half-laugh is the last piece dignity has to its back. Down beneath the green leaf of life negroes hang on now naked as caterpillar. But they eating the leaf. They will spread wings beautiful as butterflies, and adorn a new earth.

SHEPHERD: Trust meself to black people, I fall to ground. Root meself to obeah, I stay high. Sweet breeze blow on me.

DELLA: It don't trouble you, Shepherd, that there is a distance between the two colours which God never set?

SHEPHERD: Black people too tired to cover distance. *(Making a lewd pass at her.)* I will lie down with them.

DELLA: *(Starting to go out.)* God leave you to your ageing guts, you yard ram.

Enter LAL.

LAL: Miss Della. Tata dead.

DELLA: Dead?

LAL: As you stand there. Dead.

DELLA starts to go out.

SHEPHERD: *(Coming over to her, with a facial expression of sympathy.)* The death of a child can be the way back to faith and salvation.

DELLA says nothing, starts once more to go and he again interrupts her. She is holding back her tears.

Confess that obeah kill your son. Confess.

DELLA: Not obeah, Aaron.

SHEPHERD: *(Striking her.)* Confess.

DELLA: Not obeah.

SHEPHERD: Yes obeah kill him. *(Striking her.)* Admit to me it kill him.

DELLA: *(After a long silence.)* Not obeah.

SHEPHERD: You will come back to me, Della. If you not goin' starve or be a servant, you will have to come back and make my bed.

DELLA: Not obeah.

DELLA exits.

SHEPHERD: *(Overjoyed and enjoying a great calm.)* When I was a boy alone I used to sit beside the river. Evening come falling over my shoulder. When I look on the dark night I think it a relative. I solely belong to it. I don't command money like White Wolf, but like Jesus Christ I command life. That life, young in the pickney like a far out wave, I, Shepherd, squeeze to foam. Life far out in the pickney, but greedy and tough. How manhood would see it move in to lap experience, elbow and surge to lap experience; every inlet and strait, every bay and harbour and gulf, lap and fall back again. That searching lamp life, Shepherd darken with mind and finger and word. *(To LAL.)* You tell the people?

LAL: Yes I tell them.

SHEPHERD: Then tonight we wail for Tata.

SCENE TWO

Early evening.

DELLA is on her way home from SHEPHERD. She passes a number of children talking and playing, and when they mention TATA, she listens to them.

Thunder.

FIRST CHILD: It set up for rain.

SECOND CHILD: Storm goin' bust tonight. Me mother goin' cover up her bed with board and newspaper and make us sleep under it. The roof a-leak.

THIRD CHILD: Me mother say she never know a time when Trench Town roof don't leak. She say they leak like Trench Town people mouth.

SECOND CHILD: Trench Town people say Tata poorly.

FIRST CHILD: Let's play hopscotch in the dark.

THIRD CHILD: That's a girl's game.

FIRST CHILD: Throw taw, hop one, bend down, pick it up, rest two, spin round…

SECOND CHILD: Me 'fraid of the thunder.

THIRD CHILD: If you were like Tata you wouldn't 'fraid.

FIRST CHILD: Trench Town people say Tata dead.

SECOND CHILD: You think lightning can strike the dead?

THIRD CHILD: No, but it light them up so you can see their ghost.

SECOND CHILD: You ever see a wet ghost?

THIRD CHILD: Tata ghost will wear rompers to keep off the lightning.

SECOND CHILD: How long they say he dead now?

Drum.

FIRST CHILD: Some of Shepherd people say today.

SECOND CHILD: Hear the drum?

FIRST CHILD: Throw taw, hop one, spin round, rest one…

DELLA goes off. Drum. Dog howls.

SCENE THREE

DELLA's house.

The stage is empty, DELLA appears downstage-left, dragging herself home. JOSHIE appears upstage-left, carrying the baby, nursing it. DELLA reaches the window and leans against it, sobbing. JOSHIE hears her, puts the baby in the cot and runs out of the door to her.

JOSHIE: Mumma, why are you crying?

DELLA: Tata…

JOSHIE: Tata's all right. Miss Lal come here, tell me she hear Tata dead, so I nod. If Tata live or dead, it's our business, not hers. Simply because I nod Miss Lal carry it down the street that my brother dead. But he not dead. *(He shakes DELLA to convince her.)*

DELLA: Tata!! *(She runs into house and kneels over TATA.)*

JOSHIE: *(Following her into house.)* What make Miss Lal believe that because my brother sick he must die? If every sick fowl was a dinner, crows like them would be fat… Mumma, it wasn't as if I was joking with death.

DELLA: I hear Tata name fall dry from their tongue. Not a word of pity for him. Black baby life cheap as yam.

JOSHIE: *(Enjoying his ruse a little in spite of everything.)* They all hot with the death eh? They hear what they want to hear.

DELLA: Shepherd calling the whole yard to a burial service tonight.

JOSHIE: His dog must be dead.

DELLA: They believe him dead because you tell them.

JOSHIE: They believe him dead *(A mocking imitation of the stereotyped credulous negro.)* because Shepherd mark him for death like he mark Liza, and because with their own two ears they hear how he slip away from doctor medicine, pale and almost without a breath. *(He pauses listening to the balm-yard call.)* Tonight before the whole yard we can show Tata alive and flatten Shepherd.

DELLA: Yes. Listen. Tonight I will go to the yard as a penitent. When Shepherd has announced the death of Tata, he will be at my mercy. Joshie, this weapon we now have in our hands, we must use it.

The Balm-Yard call goes on as the lights fade and the curtain falls.

SCENE FOUR

A yard lit by candles wrapped in brown paper shades. In the background is a table covered with food – rice, chickens, rum; and to one leg of the table is tied a goat, pure black. The yard is gradually filling up, as many men as women, sitting on chairs or on the ground, many standing. A hymn, scarcely heard, is passing almost unconsciously from their lips; phrases taken up and let go again in the midst of talking, moving from one place to another, watching the food or just waiting in a vague expectancy. The hymn becomes a little fuller, then full enough to be the centre of interest, some enjoying it, some feeling it, some parodying it, some passing the time with a noise. Everybody harmonises, the basses with conscious and proud dexterity. They push out their chests. Then a beautifully wailed note from the same hymn signals the entrance of the "White Dove", the leading lady in the yard. She is VIE, dressed in white with white shoes and covered with a white veil. She sings with her eyes closed and her body limp, and moved by her, the whole yard sits in the entrancement of this long, slow hymn.

Two young men, GEORGE and RUDDY, now cycle up to the fence.

GEORGE: Ruddy, stop here a little. The old fools are jumping tonight. God's taught them to spend their wages on cheap silk and head wraps, while worms immobilize their children.

A MAN INSIDE THE YARD: *(Shouting.)* Move on, irreverent.

They are silent for a moment.

Is the music make people stay in this racket.

RUDDY: *(Starting to move off.)* Come George.

GEORGE starts making peculiar nasal noises wrecking the music.

GEORGE: Since God not hearing them, he might hear me. *(Making the noise again.)*

A MAN INSIDE THE YARD: No manners taught at your home, son?

GEORGE: No home, you old bastard.

MAN: No religion. No Lord, no God.

GEORGE: No Lord, God, Almighty, Saviour, Providence. With three persons and so many aliases it hard to catch up with him.

MAN: Blasphemer.

GEORGE: Shear your sheep, Shepherd.

RUDDY: Come, George.

MAN: No wonder you can't find work.

GEORGE: Oh, yes. Yes, Mass Sam. I don't like God so He stops me getting work.

RUDDY: Georgie, come, they will kick you down.

GEORGE: With their first pair of boots. You think I don't know.

The young men cycle away and the yard continues the hymn. It finishes.

A MAN: Look how our meeting going nicely, nicely, and those hooligans want to mash it up. They question too much.

A WOMAN: *(Saucily disagreeing.)* Yes, they question, but not this. This is a thing too stale to question. They question that some can sicken their bellies with food while the rest of us have to steal or want.

At this point the SHEPHERD enters with a red dunce-cap, a loose gown that falls just above his ankles and brown shoes.

A WOMAN: *(Swooningly.)* Let the wisdom of the Shepherd cool all argument.

SHEPHERD at first pays no attention to his audience but attends the table gravely, setting it in order. Then dramatically, he pronounces:

SHEPHERD: You can't serve two masters. Who won't credit me, can't feel my spirit. You hear rumours saying somebody dead. Tonight, somebody dead, and little by little through the night my little white goat turn black with his spirit. For he is a tormented spirit. And let all who believe not on me fear torment. *(Beginning an invocation.)* Come over spirit; melt away their little fear; sing out.

(He sings.) Me alone, me alone,
In the wilderness
Forty days and forty nights
In the wilderness.

*The yard takes up the hymn and SHEPHERD takes up collection.
Then DELLA comes in. The whole yard says "Della" in astonishment,
and there is a bubble of voices. She sings:*

DELLA: Oh my people
Turn back from the trudging road,
Turn, turn, turn,
Back from the trudging road.

*The people are dissatisfied with the presumption her song implies
and they protest: "What sort of song this?"*

SHEPHERD: Do you sing this to show penitence? Vie, sing her
a penitence song.

VIE: *(Her face covered with spite and insolence leads the yard in the
Sankey.)* Born of the water, the spirit and the blood
Thank God I'm born again.

*This is accompanied by a tremendous dance by SHEPHERD, in
which he jerks his chest and frowns as if shaking off the opposition
of devils.*

Born of the water, the spirit and the blood
Thank God I'm born again.

SHEPHERD: Confess now, obeah kill your son.

DELLA: Obeah failed.

JOSHIE enters with TATA. He is accompanied by GEORGE.

JOSHIE: Tata not dead. He here with the living.

The people crowd round JOSHIE.

GEORGE: Look like Shepherd can breed more than he can
kill.

Pause.

DELLA: Gullmaster.

SHEPHERD: The miracle of death reach out to the miracle of
resurrection and more glory to Shepherd. I raise him, for

her sake I did it. Because of her penitence. I said I would bring the white goat in for a sign, dead if Tata stay dead, alive if I raise him up. White for her sin, alive for her penitence. Now see the goat alive and Tata lives. Blessed be Shepherd. Ooh-aih

The crowd join in responses, then exit.

Now more of the simple people honour me, reverence me, respect me, feed me, obey me, bow the head when I talk, so no blotch come between my life and my dream. Power under my foot now; I bend down, raise it up and find it full in my hand. *(Holding her.)* Therefore, you must come over to me now, Della; draw away from the sweep of my hand to the shelter of my side.

DELLA: Your five fingers rest on my shoulder like claws. Take them off. You will yet be glad to crawl out this yard and leave me your mantle. I will see the beast's Shepherd's eyes weaken and fall beneath me, and then lead the yard away from obeah.

Enter several angry young men.

GEORGE: Well, Shepherd, you seem to fool Tom, Dick and Harry, but you can't fool George.

SHEPHERD: Pshaw. Time for bed now man, no time for argument.

GEORGE: Admit Shepherd, Della son put it over you.

SHEPHERD: Stand there fellow. No nearer.

A YOUNG MAN: Easy George, easy.

DELLA, excited at this support, runs out of the yard, but is too curious to go away altogether, and lingers unseen to hear what is happening.

SHEPHERD: Money you want?

GEORGE: Gentlemen, you know how many anxious people money this man collect up. You know what he planning for Della, and for the boy who, God bless him, open the people's eyes.

SHEPHERD: Leaving Della to God. Bothering with her no longer. From this night she is the easiest piece of tail in town. Go try her now.

Approval from some of the gang.

GEORGE: Time for that.

SHEPHERD: *(To GEORGE, speaking of the rest of the gang.)* But they out to romp with her. The both of them. One behind the other.

YOUNG MAN: Right. You know the ways of man.

SHEPHERD: *(Throwing money to the gang.)* Take this, buy cock soup to keep your strength up with her. She will tear you down. She a big woman.

GEORGE: Leave it Ruddy.

RUDDY: Leave me crutch. We can hold on to this and still bust him.

GEORGE: *(Sharply.)* Leave it.

RUDDY drops the money.

SHEPHERD: *(Calls into the house.)* Vie. Vie.

GEORGE: *(To SHEPHERD.)* Hear my word, ol' massa. Don't touch the son or the mother… Della, or Joshie or Tata.

SHEPHERD: Don't touch Joshie?

GEORGE: And make sure they stay alive. For if any of them dead, however they dead, even if God call them, we goin' feel is you murder them, and before you hang, beat you so you drag yourself from this yard to Vie's bed. Pick up your money.

SHEPHERD bends down and picks up the money bag, then slowly makes his way off downstage left. As he goes, the boys group themselves by DELLA at upstage-right-centre.

DELLA: *(Turning to RUDDY.)* Ruddy, take Papa G's bicycle, find your friends. Tell them Della will preach to the people. Explain to them. Be a leader to them.

DELLA turns and hurries out through the gate. The boys watch her go.

GEORGE: *(Turning to RUDDY.)* Well go on.

RUDDY: You go.

The lights fade down and the curtain falls, there is a pause and then DELLA is heard.

DELLA: And Moses, the great Egyptian, the black man, threw down the terrible idol. The golden calf that Aaron built the holy people trampled on when their eyes were opened. When their eyes were opened they sang.

DELLA sings the opening line of 'Hold Fast' and the CHORUS join in with her.

SCENE FIVE

At the close of the second chorus of 'Hold Fast', the singers repeat the last two lines fading in volume.

CHORUS: Hold fast and never let go,
Hold fast and never let go.

The lights come up revealing DELLA's house, GLORIA leaning left of the door, RUDDY seated window chair, JOSHIE on floor next to cradle at right, and GEORGE sitting on cradle stool.

GLORIA: Della preaching strong, but shut your eyes to her lip, for it trembling. She tell them the verse about the good Shepherd and beside him she compare Aaron. She say success please Aaron; success stop his fret; where he see success he is all over it like a tail wagging. Then she say

"This worshipper want worship. This candle burner, this salaam-hoarder, collect it, count it." She sounds good.

GEORGE: I talk to Jack, Sago, Freddie, Sam, Blackboy, and One-son. All of them aware of the ignorance and suffering, but you think they would come? Tomorrow glass factory opening up. It goin' to employ them.

RUDDY: You think I could raise something down there, George?

GEORGE: Some people are bitches, me son.

GEORGE exits. DELLA enters upstage-right, sees GEORGE disappearing.

DELLA: George! *(She enters the room.)* Where's Joe?

GLORIA: Joe gone down to the beach to catch the czar boat. He not going to come, Miss Della. I tell you already.

DELLA: You tell him I offer to buy his fish for him?

GLORIA: Yes.

DELLA: You lie!

GLORIA: Well, if I lie, just find somebody else.

GLORIA exits.

RUDDY: Tell you, Miss Della, what I want is bed, and the young lady's home that's due to oblige me with it. And I'm going.

RUDDY exits. DELLA turns to JOSHIE.

JOSHIE: Shepherd out to cripple me.

DELLA: Tonight the young men warn him.

JOSHIE: They can't protect me.

DELLA: Just a little while ago they nearly beat him.

JOSHIE: Nearly! You see how they desert you now.

DELLA: If Shepherd touch you it will anger all the people.

JOSHIE: I am no bait to catch Shepherd.

DELLA: Yes bait, like any man in the fight against him. Because we expose him tonight the young men are for Della, not Shepherd. Join them. If Shepherd touch you, he touch them.

JOSHIE: I phone the doctor. Tonight I goin' up there to sleep.

DELLA: I call you now to face him Joshie. Hear me. The whole yard know you are wanted. Everybody watching that Goliath. God's sent your stone and sling to save us. In the morning go out to him.

JOSHIE: Tomorrow mornin' me goin' start gardenin' work at doctor friend, Mrs. Matthews.

DELLA: Little while ago the young men were at him. They are crackling a little and we must fan them. They are the only ones now to destroy Aaron.

JOSHIE: I go to Mrs. Matthews this mornin' an' first thing she give me is a pants.

DELLA: Her son pants?

JOSHIE: Is a good trousers.

DELLA: What Mrs. Matthews' son name?

JOSHIE: Mass Herbie.

DELLA: *(With the slightest stress on the "Mass".)* Mass Herbie same size as you?

JOSHIE: I never see him. He have a boy size bat an' ball to play with when he come home from school.

DELLA: All the time Mass Herbie will take advantage of you.

JOSHIE: Doctor say I mus' go.

DELLA: But don't bother go.

JOSHIE: I hearin' what the doctor say.

DELLA: When Mass Herbie boots dirty who goin' clean them?

JOSHIE: I can't do better.

DELLA: What about your trade. Go back to your trade.

JOSHIE: Trade people too savage.

DELLA: People savage… till you teach them this, they not so savage, teach them that, they little less savage.

JOSHIE: Negroes take long to learn.

DELLA: You feel that. This is the power of the White-Wolf.

JOSHIE: You can do what you like.

DELLA: The hurt White-Wolf do me don't touch you.

JOSHIE: Doctor say we must bury it with Christian love.

DELLA: Stay here tonight, and leave in the morning.

JOSHIE: Why?

DELLA: Because I beg you, Joshie.

JOSHIE: No. I goin' outside to wash my face and hands.

JOSHIE exits.

DELLA: Leave me too, Tata; leave me for good. What is Della? A dirty frock with a half-dead baby. "A good woman" I hear you whisper, oh Lord? Joshie want goodness? He want station and power, so he sleep at White-Wolf's, while the good Della dwindles, her future wrapped up with Tata bedclothes. This useless fever will stay with you, Tata, shake and burn you till darkness come. The young men are for Della, not Shepherd. Tata, if I give you this pillow then plant the murder on Shepherd, how they would root up the tyrant… When the people hear that part of his magic is murder they will laugh and drink rum and spit obeah out. Oh, but the glutinous eye, treasure like its own pupil, the life it once lit on. Let Shepherd and the yard gorge themselves on the stenchy sin till they sicken, I won't root up my son to purge them… Oh, Almighty God, my life's in a tangle; single it out. If I'm to trudge on with my necessary purpose, reduce Tata to the unseen foetus I'd be glad to wash out.

JOSHIE re-enters.

You leavin' me, Joshie?

JOSHIE doesn't answer, but collects his things and goes.

Then take the lantern.

Exit JOSHIE.

In war young men just walk over to death; with no more thought than in a sleep they walk. So I must learn to use death to strain life clean. Tata, Tata. Good. Sleep. Life not made for use, it made in sport, and so light as it come, so light it should be wiped out. Oh, the long generations of mothers nestling sons, drag the power from my hand. How anxious to keep what breed in a dark corner stink with urine. When I whisper to the young men and they to one another how Shepherd savage to quench a son, pity will kindle in them, anger spurt up, the multitude lose their dampening fear and blaze. Run, Shepherd, from the heat of that fire. So, Tata, by death you destroy Shepherd and yet make White-Wolf less strong. Now negroes will wonder whether they should cook the food they can't eat, wash the clothes they can't wear, make the beds they can't climb into, and sleep.

She smothers TATA, and sits by the child for a long time, saying nothing. Then comes the DOCTOR's voice.

DOCTOR: *(Calling from outside.)* Della. Della. Della.

He pushes his head in at the door and, seeing her standing there looking at him, enters. She rises and moves the lamp over to the other corner of the room, so as to leave the bed in darkness.

They said you were in. Is it too late to call? Is it?

DELLA: It late, yes.

DOCTOR: I only came to collect Joshie. Did he tell you?
Didn't he say? He wanted to stay at my house tonight. I
invited him. Unless you object.

DELLA: Joshie gone.

DOCTOR: What is it? What's wrong? You don't look very well.
You're trembling. Mind if I close the door? I can't leave
here with you sick. Unless you insist.

DELLA doesn't answer, but he goes on talking, talking, talking.

(Going up to DELLA.) Why don't you let me stay and look
after you for a bit?

DELLA: You hold me like this because I sick.

DOCTOR: I'm sorry. I guessed that's what you were afraid of.
(He settles DELLA down to chat.) Last night I dreamt I had
my office in the yard out there and the people around
came swarming, but somehow I was only sitting down, and
it was Joshie going among them healing. Do dreams mean
a lot to you?

DELLA: I never remember them.

DOCTOR: But suppose I did set up shop and came to live
down here. Would it surprise you? I have done things on
impulse. But would you – White Wolf and all that – want
me to? Would you? Rent me one of these same 12/- a
month things. Keep it clean. No more or better furniture
than the neighbours have. You'd cook for me, wouldn't
you? A garden, such as they could have if they bothered.
And I'd soon have Shepherd as a patient.

DELLA makes no reply.

If I did come and set up shop, would you come and live
with me then?

DELLA's thoughts are elsewhere.

DELLA: Doctor?

DOCTOR: You used to say "doctor" in that way only when I wasn't welcome. How's Tata? Still in my care?

DOCTOR goes to cot.

Let's have a look at him.

DOCTOR goes to pick up the lamp.

DELLA: Give me.

DELLA takes the lamp and goes to cot, followed by the Doctor.

DOCTOR: *(Sees TATA's swollen dead face.)* Was Aaron here?

DELLA: Yes. I come in and find him here.

DOCTOR: The people outside said you haven't been out all evening. *(After a pause, turning on her.)* I see. Didn't you even love your son?

DELLA: *(With some sarcasm.)* Won't the angels receive him?

DOCTOR: If word gets out to the police, Della, I couldn't see Shepherd hang.

DELLA: You bleed for Aaron?

DOCTOR: Bury Tata quietly. I'll certify. He died. No one killed him. Not you, nor Shepherd.

DELLA: Bury him? I watch him kick when I press him.

DOCTOR: It isn't a cheap decision. There's danger for me in it. If I don't report murder I am an accomplice.

DELLA: I tear out a path I must follow. If I hang I am with him.

LAL: *(From outside.)* Miss Della? *(She enters.)*

DOCTOR: Jesus Christ!

LAL: Only in the darkness I venture in to the street.

DELLA: You come to hear how you stand with Shepherd?

LAL: Della! That man mother suckle him with gall, and the rest of us must burn and laugh and suffer at his will, and be the sheep that Shepherd can kill.

DELLA: And now, who kill Tata, Lal?

LAL: Tata gone? I didn't know your grief was so dear.

DELLA: Before you sleep, go round Trench Town and say Shepherd murder Tata, Della son.

LAL: I will tell the people that Shepherd sent me the other day to murder Tata.

LAL exits door.

DELLA: You will go to the police and defeat me now.

DOCTOR: If word gets out to the police, Della...

DELLA: Word won't get to the police. We won't bother with the police. The police are nearly asleep now, but the people are waking. *(She goes to cradle.)* Tonight, all round your body they will wail, then march on Shepherd.

DOCTOR: Will they? You really believe that?

DELLA: When the light in my eyes strike the multitude of mourners, their tears, like blades will glitter.

The DOCTOR exits. DELLA sinks onto stool. LAL hurries across the stage from wing to wing and small groups begin to whisper offstage. One by one six women and a little girl enter to commiserate with DELLA and form a group round the cradle. First lady goes off left for a candle and returns, second lady begins to sing 'Rock of Ages'. The others join in. Two more ladies go off and return with two candles each. On the end of the line "Be of sin" the lights fade and the curtain falls.

SCENE SIX

An hour later, children are still awake and talking.

A bell.

FIRST CHILD: Catholic bell ring late.

SECOND CHILD: *(Bell.)* Only some o' the stroke the breeze blow over.

FIRST CHILD: It sound slow, like a death bell.

SECOND CHILD: Death for my litter of rabbits. All tonight I hear them whisper 'bout Tata.

FIRST CHILD: Women su-su like the breeze in a cashaw tree.

SECOND CHILD: All tonight Della preach against the obeah man, but the people don't have any heart. They 'fraid.

FIRST CHILD: Your Aunt Jane 'fraid.

SECOND CHILD: Yes.

FIRST CHILD: And I'm afraid.

SECOND CHILD: Only some of the strokes the breeze blow over, an' it sound like death.

Bell louder.

SCENE SEVEN

As the light gets brighter, more and more people are revealed.

SHEPHERD: You feel I do murder. I do no murder, but you draw round to stare at me like a murderer. Is twenty of you and me one. Why you having mercy then on me? Because you know that if there is murder, the court is not in Della's back yard, but in the town.

Faint murmurs of approval.

You will wait till I am charged.

Louder murmurs.

Till then you will count me a murderer, or the keeper of the commandment, "Thou shalt do no murder"?

GEORGE: *(Shouting interruptions.)* You didn't send Lal the other day to murder Tata.

SHEPHERD: If Tata dead, I didn't kill him.

GEORGE: You escaped from your guilt, now your innocence should hang you.

SHEPHERD: *(To the crowd.)* He knows I am innocent.

GEORGE: I know you sent Lal after Tata the other day. And plenty of these people here know. *(To the people.)* Some of you *know* that the other day he sent Miss Lal to murder Tata.

A WOMAN'S VOICE IN THE CROWD: Yes.

GEORGE: *(To the crowd.)* And many of you know that the miracle tonight was a sham.

SHEPHERD: *(Calling for someone to chuck GEORGE out.)* Frank!

GEORGE: *(Shouting SHEPHERD down.)* Hear me. Where is the miracle that will put away our hunger?

A MAN IN THE CROWD: *(One of SHEPHERD's cronies.)* Hunger not everything. Hunger is nothing. The thing is to drag the woman Della here to preach white supremacy in Trench Town. That would bring the white man in to be Lord and God.

SHEPHERD: Yes, when the power of God is living black.

GEORGE opens his mouth to answer and is struck across it. In the excitement, SHEPHERD whips up the crowd.

Someone murder Tata. God will forgive everything except to the man with blood on his hands. Why? Because all sin, and fall short of the glory, and to repent, God gives us his chosen number of years and no man must cut them off.

That is why, though Della charging this and that, you sit cold and wait. Wait for me to talk, to hear me.

Approval from the CROWD.

Not all that cry "Lord, Lord" shall enter, nor all that point the finger are guiltless. If she cry, "Murderer", she must have a witness. And who is that witness?

Isolated cries of "None!"

Frank, go to the police and say Shepherd reporting murder in Trench Town. The good book says judge no man. No man at all. Call no man murderer. *(He lowers his voice and is sardonic.)* And you read no man except Aaron.

WOMAN'S VOICE: *(Ecstatically.)* Frank is on his way to the police station.

SHEPHERD: What this woman, Della, have, oh Lord, that they should swallow her word and reject me. Come and hear from me the little dignity I walk in, at her word. Suppose the police come on at me, and truncheon me till I bring out tears. That woman is without justice and have no mercy. And for any such, oh Lord, correction. Yes, for any such. Do unto others as they would do unto thee.

There is a great excitement and echoing of his words.

Do ye even so to them. Yes. Go to her house and drag her here. Make her confess I am no murderer.

The crowd pick up the last words of the SHEPHERD 'Drag her out' and begin to chant them working up to a frenzy. Three of the men disappear off upstage-right through the gate, the drums pick up the rhythm. When the noise is at its height the men appear at the gate dragging DELLA with them. They throw her down at SHEPHERD's feet. The crowd fall silent.

GEORGE: *(As they throw her down.)* No! Ruddy! No!

PAPA G: Bitch.

DELLA drags herself up and turns to the crowd who, blocking her path of escape, shout and scream at her. Desperate, she turns to the SHEPHERD, sees the knife in his belt and grabs it. The crowd, horrified suddenly fall silent and back away from her. Before anyone can stop her she throws herself at SHEPHERD, who tries in vain to evade her, and stabs him several times in the back The crowd scream.

GEORGE: *(Shouting.)* No, Miss Dell, Miss Dell! No!

The SHEPHERD screams, staggers and falls, DELLA backs to the left pros-arch. There is silence. GEORGE kneels by the body, crosses to DELLA. LAL enters upstage right.

LAL: The police out there. The Doctor bring them in his car.

Enter DOCTOR and JOSHIE. The DOCTOR stoops by the body of the SHEPHERD and examines him, he finds him dead, all eyes turn to watch DELLA.

DELLA: Look like guilt alone just didn't have the edge for killing a man. He was the law down here, and there seemed no power in Heaven to sentence him. It please God that some should ride and some fall under. *(She starts to go, pauses by JOSHIE.)* Bury Tata. *(As she goes, the curtain slowly falls.)*

SKYVERS

Skyvers: an appreciation

When I first came across *Skyvers* in 1970, it struck me as a powerful, relevant and hugely articulate work. I knew it had already been produced at the Royal Court some eight years before but I was running the Young People's Scheme there at that time and they agreed to a second production.

The gap, cultural, social and economic between the working class, or do we now call them the underclass, and the middle/upper class is a chasm. It is the running sore through our society and it amazes me how little it is written about. *Skyvers* was one of the first plays I ever read that really laid it out. In 1971 when I directed it, it was painfully astute; in 2007, when it was revived for a reading as part of the 50th anniversary season at The Royal Court, it remained painfully astute and relevant.

How had Barry, a Jamaican teacher, in a London comprehensive, described so accurately the alienation and rage of south London boys? The entrapment of both boys and girls bounded by sex, violence and either dull dead-end jobs or crime was described so perfectly by Barry. He had come to England, had gone to Cambridge but was black, radical and incapable of compromise. He had a ringside at what social alienation meant.

The class differences at work in most schools is particularly intense in secondary modern schools. The expectations are virtually nil, the teachers soon worn down. But the social differences have to be preserved, the rituals of middle class life: good behaviour, obedience, politeness, have got to be preserved. Only the young, still idealistic supply teacher, is prepared to not to waste time imposing rules of behaviour in the hope of discovering some positives in his class of apparent hoodlums.

Cragge, the hero of the piece, (superbly played by Michael Kitchen), is football mad, he has a notion of becoming a professional player or writing about it for the school paper. He struggles not to get dragged down by the nihilism of his peers. But ultimately fails.

John Lennon's best song *Working Class Hero* has the lines, 'they hate you if you're clever, they despise the fool.' *Skyvers* explores this contradiction that paralyses loads of working class kids. If you're clever at school, then you're going over to their side, you're adopting their standards and their world. No one wants to be seen to be doing that, so you have to excel in strictly working class ways: fighting, sexual aggrandisement, crime, if you're a boy. Sexual allure and power, if you're a girl. It's exactly this hopeless contradiction that Barry writes so well about, all the kids in *Skyvers* are being destroyed by it.

Skyvers was produced in Sloane Square in 1971, hardly the appropriate habitat for it. I was reminded of its in-appropriateness in 2007, when on the first morning of rehearsal for the revived reading, I paused at the window of a furnishing store and looked at a garden bench for sale at £600.

Back in 1971 we had to bus in kids from the same background as the kids in *Skyvers* and they loved it. When it transferred to the huge space in The Roundhouse the excitement among the young audience was palpable as the kids in the play crashed their desks around. *Skyvers* asked them the right questions: what was being done to them and what were they doing to themselves. *Skyvers* was a hit. It didn't go into the West End or make any money but it was seen by the right audiences.

I think of all those 1960s, 1970s writers Barry was one of the very best. He wrote cogently and imaginatively about the world we lived in. Why is he not more rated and more successful? Well he didn't play any of the games, he is intelligent and his plays demanded change. Whether you were black or white didn't matter... didn't matter if you were poor, alienated. If your life had never had a chance to begin then the world had to change so you could be part of it. And British theatre has never really been interested in change, in genuine equality: Barry is and that's why British theatre has found it so hard to give him his place.

Pam Brighton

Skyvers was first performed on the 23rd July 1963 at the Royal Court Theatre, London, directed by Ann Jellicoe with the following cast:

CRAGGE, David Hemmings (Michael Kitchen)
BROOK, Phillip Martin (Joe Blatchley)
COLMAN, Nicholas Edmett (Mike Gredy)
ADAMS, John Hall (Billy Hamon)
JORDAN, Lance Kaufman (Jonathan Bagnor)
FREEMAN, Bernard Kay (William Hoyland)
WEBSTER, John Woodnutt (Len Tentan)
HEADMASTER, Dallas Caval (Len Tentan)
HELEN, Chloe Ashcroft (Cheryl Hall)
SYLVIA, Annette Robertson (Pam Scotcher)

The names in brackets are for the 1971 production at the Royal Court Theatre directed by Pam Brighton.

Editor's note: *Skyvers* appears to have has been updated in every production it has received. The version selected is from the first performance as the essence of the play is cogent enough for it to stand as originally written.

Characters

CRAGGE

BROOK

COLMAN

ADAMS

JORDAN

Fifteen-year-old boys in a school

FREEMAN

WEBSTER

HEADMASTER

Masters

HELEN

SYLVIA

Fifteen-year-old girls

Preface

Although I have avoided any artificially heightened language and kept within the range of cockney idiom, the language in this play is clearly invented. Schoolboys, on the whole don't talk in the way I make them talk. Usually their talk is less interesting. But if the play sounds real it is because I've got down what these boys do in fact think and feel, although often they are too inarticulate to say it. This, to me, is the imaginative process – the whole business of writing.

People emerge whole only when you capture convincingly their thoughts and feelings. When I hear their actual speech, it often seems too trivial to be in any way important. But this is obviously only its surface. It is the writer's imagination that takes us beneath it, and by showing the whole person makes him invaluable.

This is a very different thing from documentary or naturalism, which I would define as the capturing of surface reality. Writers always want to get away from the surface. They want to reflect the underbelly of feeling, and in the attempt always have to face the crucial question of speech. They all have to heighten speech, but how? Do they heighten in within the common idiom, or do they go outside it, use phrases that people would never say, *artificially* heighten? This is in one form or another the underlying debate in recent drama. What is heightened speech? It is an old question, but absolutely crucial. For me, heightened speech is ordinary speech which is at the same time perceptive – the kind of thing one could put quite naturally into the mouth of some old cockney Lear: 'I'll do things… What, I don't know… I'll be a terror'. The best word for this is realism, and realism should never be confused with naturalism. The distinction is useful. Naturalistic speech is ordinary which is commonplace. Realistic speech sounds like ordinary speech but it has to be invented to convey an area of experience which is not on the surface.

The danger of realism is that whatever sounds like the language of ordinary people will always, in a thoughtless way, be taken to be commonplace. Also, in a snobbish way. In England those accents are thought the ugliest which are identified with the poorest people. Also, in the court of public opinion, which goes on broad impressions, one must not only invent but be seen to invent. But of course artificial heightening needs no more invention than realism. Besides, the realistic writer avoids the prevalent dangers of artificial heightening: routine repetition, rhythm, assonance; and in working within the mould of people's speech retains checks and balances without which he might so easily drift into consecrated banalities about life, death and love.

Barry Reckord

Act One

SCENE ONE

Outside the school. It's early and there's nobody around except CRAGGE, who is waiting for HELEN to pass. He is always glancing up the road till he glimpses her coming and moves away, not wanting to be seen too obviously waiting; but he stays in full view so she can see him.

Enter HELEN.

CRAGGE: What's the hurry?

HELEN: Some people have to work. Look at you, bloody boots, holding up the school gate.

CRAGGE: I'm in a match at the school here tonight.

HELEN: Where's your mates?

CRAGGE: Round somewhere. Colley'll be here in a minute.

HELEN: Was you waiting for me to pass the school here last night?

CRAGGE: What happened to you then?

HELEN: Was busy.

CRAGGE: Oh?

HELEN: Sylvia says she saw you hanging round.

Helen starts to exit.

CRAGGE: Helen.

HELEN: I gotta get to work. I been late three mornings this week.

CRAGGE: I'm outta school for good three weeks time. *(Solemnly.)* Pay for you at the flicks then.

HELEN: You're gonna take me out!

CRAGGE: When I start workin'. I'll have the money then.

HELEN: Take me out sometime never.

CRAGGE: It's why I'm leavin'.

HELEN: You won't get much. I've been out three months workin' hard as hell for me livin' and not seein' where the money's going to. I suppose I see where it's goin'. I enjoy meself.

Whistle off.

Who's that?

CRAGGE: It's Colley comin' to give me a massage.

HELEN: Where's Brooksie then?

CRAGGE: Brook ain't my mate.

HELEN: O ain't 'e? What's massage?

CRAGGE: Loosens up your muscles for a match. You got to be fit and you got to be padded. I have on me thick socks see? Look! And I'll line them with a pair of exercise books so I'm padded round here... and boots get greased for a big match. Chelsea's sending over a talent scout.

HELEN: What 'appened to that rock 'n roll contest you was in Saturday.

CRAGGE: Come around fifth or sixth but I ain't really interested any more now. The bastards who put me in sixth said I wasn't good enough, yet one judge said I was best so where are ya?

HELEN: Didn't Colley whistle? Why doesn't he come?

CRAGGE: Don't know.

HELEN: Is he with someone?

CRAGGE: Who?

HELEN: I don't know.

CRAGGE: Who did you think?

HELEN: No one.

CRAGGE: Brook.

HELEN: You need football and rock 'n roll to shine. Other blokes have themselves.

CRAGGE: Who d'ya mean?

HELEN: Well, your mates ain't always performin'. Brook can just talk ordinary to people.

CRAGGE: 'Ave you been getting acquainted with Brook?

HELEN: Has anyone been saying I have?

CRAGGE: Well have you?

HELEN: I asked you first.

CRAGGE: 'E ain't much good at anything.

HELEN: Sez you!

CRAGGE: What about coming to see the match tonight? Then after we could do something.

HELEN: I might.

CRAGGE: If Brook's going.

HELEN: Is he going?

CRAGGE: Was it him you was out with last night?

HELEN: What if I was?

CRAGGE: You don't want to get mixed up with Brook. Saw 'im the other night with some tart. Disgusting.

HELEN: Doin' what?

CRAGGE: Was 'e touching you last night?

HELEN: No.

CRAGGE: On your hon?

HELEN: Yes.

CRAGGE: Say on your honour.

HELEN: On my honour... Disgustin' doin' what?

CRAGGE: You don't want to be at the mercy of the likes of him.

HELEN: Don't I?

CRAGGE: If it's him you're hangin' around for you should hear what he'll say about you.

HELEN: Well, I'll worry when I hear him saying it, not you.

CRAGGE: Did he put his arm round you last night? *(He touches her.)*

HELEN: Hey.

CRAGGE: I just wanted to see how far you let him.

HELEN: 'I just wanted to see how far you let him!' You get my wick. You're bottom of my list for going out and top a no one's.

CRAGGE: Brook is top, though.

HELEN: Yes he is. When he talks to a girl his hand ain't all sweaty to hold from being nervous.

CRAGGE: When he talks to you you're timid as bloody 'ell and laugh at any old rubbish he says.

HELEN: No girl would 'ave you if she could get him.

CRAGGE: Yeah, the world's full a dunces!

HELEN: No girl will 'ave nothing to do with you 'cos you're square as 'ell, and next time you touch me I'll 'ave your bloody eyes.

Enter COLMAN.

COLMAN: Hello

HELEN: Hello Colley.

CRAGGE: Hello.

COLMAN: *(To CRAGGE.)* Brooksie's in the caff. Wants us there.

HELEN: 'As 'e got a cuppa ready for us then?

COLMAN: Ask 'im.

CRAGGE: What about your work then?

HELEN: Oh –

CRAGGE: What's the time, Colley?

HELEN: Oh, I can stop for a cuppa. *(Exit HELEN.)*

COLMAN: You comin'?

CRAGGE: You go wiv 'im.

COLMAN: Come on, it's Brook.

CRAGGE: Yeah so you go on wiv 'im.

COLMAN: Your old man 'it you?... I'll give you a quick one.

CRAGGE: School's open.

SCENE TWO

Follows immediately.

Classroom.

COLMAN: Get old Barker's table, eh?

CRAGGE: O.K. *(Exit and re-enter with table.)* Good game last
night.

COLMAN: Great.

CRAGGE: Last ten minutes couldn't get hold of the bleeding
ball.

COLMAN: Smashing goal that last one.

CRAGGE: You know where I took that shot? Right in the middle of the instep.

COLMAN: I heard blokes say you might play inside left. If it's fine by tonight there ought to be a bit of a crowd.

CRAGGE: Use Vaseline.

COLMAN: I got linament. The real players use linament.

CRAGGE: What d'you mean, real?

They start the massage.

COLMAN:They're putting up the nets for tonight.

CRAGGE: Yeah, going to be muddy as hell.

COLMAN: D'you think you'll be in the team?

CRAGGE: It'll be a brand new ball.

COLMAN: You can borrow my shin guards if you like.

CRAGGE: Miles Davis the trumpeter says he corrects his own faults.

COLMAN: What's Miles Davis got to do with football?

CRAGGE: I let mine slide.

Enter BROOK.

BROOK: Massage!

COLMAN: Did you see 'Elen?

BROOK: Yeah, she come into the caff. I made 'er late as 'ell. You comin'?

CRAGGE: Finish me Colley!

BROOK: Stay if you like.

CRAGGE: Colley!

COLMAN: Brooksie's 'ere.

BROOK: Are you comin'?

CRAGGE: 'E's only just started. (*To COLLEY.*) 'E ain't in the match tonight.

COLMAN: I'll finish 'im quick.

BROOK: Then am I gonna stand 'ere watchin'?

CRAGGE: Just because you ain't playin'!

BROOK: You mightn't even be playin'. The team ain't up yet.

COLMAN: 'Is name's in the first thirteen.

BROOK: 'Is name's in the first thirteen but only eleven blokes play.

COLMAN: 'E was best on the field last night.

BROOK: Best on the field my sister's fanny. All season you've been only second eleven. Second eleven all season.

CRAGGE: Because they pick blokes who the bleedin' headmaster likes and the headmaster likes them that don't swear…

COLMAN: Don't smoke and don't eat in the street.

CRAGGE: What's swearin' got to do with football?

BROOK: The old boy can't play a bloke who'll go into decent people's pavilions droppin' blue lights can he? 'E'd lose the manor.

CRAGGE: You're his mate, ain't you?

BROOK: 'E's all right. If you know they mightn't put you on the side 'cos of swearing you're a big nit to go on swearin' ain't you.

CRAGGE: What has swearing got to do with football?

BROOK: But it might keep you off the side yet you go on doing it. You queer your own pitch don't you?

CRAGGE: Apes, bloody dunces and apes.

Pause.

Old Barker wanted me for this match... swearing an all, but 'e's off sick. That's my luck... Where's justice?

COLMAN: Old Barker says 'e's quite good and needs encouragement.

CRAGGE: Quite good my arse. I come from low down in the school so I'm quite good. If I came from the sixth I'd be a bloody genius...

BROOK: Anyway it's only a schoolboy match... Ain't Spurs *v.* Fulham.

CRAGGE: This bloke's discovered America.

COLMAN laughs and goes on massaging.

BROOK. *(Trying to recoup.)* Spurs gonna win, anyway.

COLMAN: We're backing Fulham.

BROOK: They won't win.

COLMAN: *(Feebly.)* They will.

BROOK: They won't.

COLMAN: *(Backing down, to CRAGGE's fury.)* I don't know, really.

CRAGGE: Fat lot a good just saying they will they won't. Depends if Fulham is fit, don't it?

BROOK: It says in the *Mirror* this mornin' they ain't fit, don't it, Colley?

COLMAN doesn't commit himself.

CRAGGE: One paper says that, another says different.

BROOK: You're a brain box, ain't you?

CRAGGE: The papers say different things. You ignorant nana. One says one thing another says different.

BROOK: It's luck wins a football match.

CRAGGE: All right then…

BROOK: *(Interrupting.)* You see 'em evenly matched yet one wins. It's a bleedin' lot a luck every time.

CRAGGE: Listen to what I'm sayin'…

BROOK: Like Fulham winning last week, that was luck.

COLMAN: *(To BROOK regretfully.)* The papers said it was fitness.

BROOK: *(Coming round unconsciously to CRAGGE's point in a rage.)* The papers say different things, one paper says that, another says different.

COLMAN: Yeah that's true.

CRAGGE: That's what I said. *(Viciously, to COLMAN.)* Didn't you hear me say it you weak-headed bum.

COLMAN: *(A bit sheepish.)* You're the big 'ead ain't ya?

CRAGGE: Well he come round to what I say, didn't he?

BROOK: Blimey! They'll be so supple them legs, they'll be kickin' both ways. Colley, let 'im 'ave 'is bloody match and let's go up to Soho tonight.

CRAGGE: Tonight's the match. You can go up to Soho any night.

COLMAN: *(To CRAGGE.)* It was a rotten swiz we paid twelve and six for that time. Why don't we try for a quid.

BROOK: How about it, Craggsie?

COLMAN: *(To CRAGGE.)* After the match.

CRAGGE: D'you think paying twice as much means they strip right down to the niff.

COLMAN: 'E can't afford a quid. His dad's hard up.

BROOK: Dunno about his dad. E's as tight as a crab's arse and that is watertight.

CRAGGE: Look, we've seen it once. You won't see no more in Soho for a quid than you see for three and six in the flicks. The only difference is in Soho you'll get coppers asking 'ow old you are.

BROOK: You teether. *(To COLMAN.)* Let's push.

CRAGGE: *(Fighting.)* Push nothing. *(To BROOK.)* Three weeks time I'll be getting as much money as you 'cos we'll 'ave the same wages.

BROOK: 'Ow much do you think my uncle's gonna pay me to 'elp 'im run 'is garage?

CRAGGE: It ain't 'is garage. 'E only works there.

BROOK: Who's bleedin' uncle is it any'ow?

CRAGGE: Bein' your uncle don't make it 'is garage.

COLMAN: *(To CRAGGE.)* He runs it.

CRAGGE: If your uncle runs it why does he clean bloody cars?

BROOK: 'E cleans bloody cars, I won't.

CRAGGE: You'll be a mechanic. Mucky as 'ell. All over grease. Fingers. Hands. Ugh. You'll never be clean.

BROOK: D'you think I'm gonna spend my life being a mechanic making a few lousy nicker a week. I'll sell second-hand cars on the side. I'll make thousands doin' that. You wait till I start pinchin' cars myself and floggin' 'em. File off the engine number. Swap the chassis.

CRAGGE: That'll be the day.

BROOK: I nicked that motor-bike and flogged it, didn't I? You start on little jobs and work up to the big. I'm gonna be the biggest. And the great ones never get caught. They're king.

COLMAN: What about people losin' hard-earned money from thievin'?

BROOK: If they're poor they're still poor. But a gang aren't half rich. They ain't earnin' twenty quid a week in a dead-end job. Their kids go to fee-payin' private schools not to great work-houses like this. Rubbin' shoulders wiv Clore's son. Richer than Clore 'cos there's no tax on it. And they ain't only rich, they're known. If you ain't got their name you ain't as good as them, no matter how honest.

CRAGGE: Yeah, they got a name; rammin' vans in daylight, bashin' up the old blokes in 'em.

BROOK: It's nerve and brain. Thinkin' it up, plannin' it, then doin' it there in broad daylight in the open street and not leavin' off till you've bagged every tanner. And when you think what they planned mightn't be what's wantin' – some geezer might have narked or a little word goes wrong and it's a stretch in store for 'em. But they ain't spendin' their life like you're gonna be doin' makin' ten quid a week on a building site and havin' to fight off them blacks and the Irish.

COLMAN: Wot if 'e's a famous footballer fightin' off fans then? Runnin' a natty little sports job and busy as 'ell with the wimmen.

BROOK: Wimmen! Do me a favour! What about me and Helen.

COLMAN: *(To BROOK.)* You got off wiv 'Elen?

There is a banging of a bell for the first period.

CRAGGE: *(Shouting above the bell.)* Girls ain't gonna make you a livin'.

COLMAN: Did you then?

BROOK: Ask me no questions, Colley boy, and I'll tell you no lies.

COLMAN: Oh, go on, tell.

JORDAN and ADAMS enter. CRAGGE wants to keep off the subject of HELEN.

CRAGGE: What do we 'ave this period. *(He looks busily at COLMAN's timetable.)*

JORDAN: *(A lout.)* Dunno.

CRAGGE: English. But old Barker's away.

ADAMS: *(A small boy; drily.)* Bet 'e's left for good. The good 'uns go, the 'orrible ones keep.

COLMAN: *(To BROOK.)* Did you scratch Helen?

CRAGGE: *(To JORDAN.)* Have you seen about any sort of job for when you leave, or are you gonna be poncin'?

BROOK: Football fills his bloody head so he give the teachers nothing but trouble at school. And last cricket season there was 'im at the wicket, one hand on his bat, the other over his eyes, prayin'.

CRAGGE: Concentratin'.

BROOK: Makin' a big score meant so much to him he was prayin'.

CRAGGE: Makin' a big score means you get a good paper from 'em when you're leavin'. You gotta kiss 'em till you can kick 'em.

BROOK: Bet you'll be borrowin' Colley's boots this evenin'.

CRAGGE: I never thought my borrowin' a pair of boots gets talked about.

BROOK: Ain't only boots. It's spikes, everything, ain't it, Colley.

CRAGGE: All right, because I do everything.

COLMAN: *(To CRAGGE.)* 'Ave you done 'Elen?

BROOK: *(Lewd.)* 'E done 'imself. Cost 'im nothing. *(Loud laughter.)*

JORDAN: *(Discovering a slogan.)* Do it yourself. Fantastic.

CRAGGE: If we stay quiet we might 'ave a free period.

JORDAN: Listen to 'im. He wants a paper from the headmaster.

CRAGGE: You need a good word from 'em to get a good job.

BROOK: Wot's the good of a paper. The bloody Irish foreman can't read any'ow.

ADAMS: If you get a paper from them, they let you dig the pavement instead of the road.

COLMAN: *(To CRAGGE.)* Them blokes cleanin' windows say you could get one a them jobs easy.

BROOK: *(To CRAGGE.)* Why not 'ave one a them. *(Nasty.)* It's honest.

CRAGGE: *(Laughing it off.)* Cleanin' school windows. You couldn't never see four bare legs in a bed.

BROOK: Yeah, you don't get a chance nickin' much, window cleanin' a school.

CRAGGE: It ain't interestin' neither. Come day go day. God send Sunday.

BROOK: You don't 'ave to stick it. No one sticks it.

CRAGGE: No. You can move on to pressin' washers. All day the same little round washer instead of all day the same big square window. Who's done them homework sums? *(He glances at COLMAN's book.)*

COLMAN: No copyin'.

CRAGGE: I can do 'em.

COLMAN: Well then, do 'em.

CRAGGE: What's one over five plus two over seven in the winged brackets. They don't mean nutten.

COLMAN: *(Sarcastic, over-simplifying.)* One over five is a fifth. Like four shillings is a fifth of a pound. One seventh of a guinea is three shillings. Two sevenths is twice that. Six shillings.

CRAGGE: And you gotta find L.C.M. you bloody fool. I know about that. But them brackets.

COLMAN: And L.C.M. is least common multiple.

ADAMS: *(Mocking CRAGGE.)* 'Ave an apple.

CRAGGE: All right. So what's a multiple then?

COLMAN: 'Ow do you mean?

CRAGGE: What's a multiple?

COLMAN: I don't know what a multiple is. I know 'ow to do L.C.M.

CRAGGE: You don't understand what you're doin' but you're doin' it. *(For a second he feels this victory justifies his doing nothing.)*

BROOK: *(To CRAGGE.)* Who's gamblin'?

CRAGGE: *(Resolution forgotten.)* For 'alfpennies?

BROOK: Pennies.

CRAGGE: 'Alfpennies.

BROOK: Whoever plays with my cards plays for pennies.

CRAGGE: I gotta do this writin' any'ow. *(Now he really settles down.)*

BROOK: Resolution Jim. I'm layin' odds you write nothin'.

CRAGGE: It's on.

JORDAN: *(Out of the blue.)* A do-it-yourself kit. Why did I never think of it. Get one cheap from Japan. *(The boys laugh.)*

BROOK: Japs. The yellow bastards. *(To the others.)* Did you see *Son of Dracula* the other night?

ADAMS: No, nor 'is old man neither.

CRAGGE: *(Looking up briefly from his sums to mock the weak joke.)* Ha, ha.

BROOK: … this bloke caught snoopin' y'see. 'E's a spy and 'e knows what the price is. 'E knows 'e'll 'ave 'is tongue out so 'e can't tell what 'e's seen.

CRAGGE is making what effort he can in spite of BROOK's babble.

So when they start workin' on 'im – tyin' 'im down, they strap 'im to a table like – when they start on 'im the poor bastard screams like 'e's 'aving babies and swears 'e'll work on their side instead. They 'ad 'im where they wanted 'im. They just look at 'im till 'e gets very jumpy. Then one of them says to 'im that 'e's a two-faced bastard and they say, 'you two-faced twister we'll give you two tongues as well'. So they 'old 'is tongue and slice it down the middle.

CRAGGE: *(Trying to concentrate.)* Belt up.

COLMAN: Did they show 'em slicin' 'im?

BROOK: They didn't show all of it. But you saw the startin' off like. And you know they done it because for the rest of the picture the bloke couldn't make nothin' but a dumb noise. *(Imitates the noise. The boys laugh.)*

CRAGGE: *(Looking up from his sums.)* I wouldn't pay five bob for that.

BROOK: Why?

CRAGGE: *(Looking up again; pointing at JORDAN's book.)* 'Cos the Japs do worse. They slit your eyeballs and chew 'em. Unless you're a woman.

ADAMS: What do they do to the women?

COLMAN: They just leave 'em to Cragge.

ADAMS: *(Going down on his knees, his hands clasped, his voice fervent.)* Why didn't they leave 'em to me?

BROOK: You don't 'ave what it takes.

CRAGGE: I 'eard in prayers last night that Chelsea's sending over a talent scout.

BROOK: *(To CRAGGE.)* You can't wait can you? *(To the others.)* 'E'll be killin' time till then.

CRAGGE: *(With absolute self-confidence.)* If I'm playin' well I'm best on the side...

BROOK: One match.

JORDAN: *(Affectionately to CRAGGE.)* Big 'ead.

BROOK: *(Utter scorn.)* Professional footballer! £65,000 transfer man.

CRAGGE: What I 'ave which the talent scout can't miss is a body swerve which no one else in the side 'as, 'ardly. I don't always get it. I get it when... *(Wiggling with anxiety.)* Dunno 'ow I get it. But if I'm on form and it 'appens I stand a good chance. The trouble is I've never played well twice running, so perhaps bein' good tonight won't make no difference.

ADAMS: What 'appens if they spot you?

CRAGGE: Dunno. Then I shouldn't 'ave to worry about no paper from no 'eadmaster. My legs'll be insured for a few hundred thousand like old Stan Matthews.

JORDAN: *(Embracing CRAGGE with admiration.)* Stanley Matthews.

CRAGGE: Stan! Stan fusses about too much. And 'e don't often drive to goal from right out on the wing. *(Then begins a dramatic account that gradually brings the others crowding around.)* A good pass to centre would do instead of all this dodging about on the wing. 'E's a crowd pleaser, Stan Matthews. I wanna develop a kinda lob that goes right over the bleedin' defence and drops right on the centre forward's boot and then it's up to 'im, in't it? I done my job. I want that lob and this is what I want again. Just look at this. Ball over to me. I'm dribblin' down the line, beat the left half about thirty yards out the area; instead of waitin' to draw more defence, slowing the game down, holding up the forward line, I shoot. From right where I am. Right out.

ADAMS: From thirty yards out!

CRAGGE: I shoot, low and hard, from thirty yards out. And not to the far side of the goal, either. No cross-shot that they might dive and save. But on my side. Just inside the upright.

COLMAN: *(Excited.)* If anyone can develop that and the lob 'e'd be the bloody best in England.

BROOK: Five hundred years' time! What about me last night.?

ADAMS: What about you last night?

BROOK: Last night I borrowed me uncle's motor bike. And 'ad 'Elen on the back, 'ugging me round the midriff… and then what?

COLMAN: You got off wiv 'Elen?

CRAGGE: Liar.

BROOK: I done 'er.

COLMAN: 'Ave you?

BROOK: Twice. She made me swear I wouldn't tell so don't tell her I told you.

CRAGGE: *(Unable to bear this detail.)* Liar!

BROOK: Sez you who knows nothin' about nothin'. *(Pointing to CRAGGE.)* 'E dunno 'ow it works. 'Is mind's all blurry about it. She said when 'e mucked about wiv 'er 'e couldn't do nothin'.

COLMAN: *(To CRAGGE.)* You let on to me you learnt off 'er, you liar.

CRAGGE: 'E knows everythin' don't 'e.

COLMAN: There was the two of us talkin' about it and neither of us done it.

CRAGGE: *(Beating the air.)* What a lie. What a damn liar.

COLMAN: *(Laughing against CRAGGE.)* 'E used to go out of 'is way to cycle past my sister but didn't 'ave the guts to talk to 'er. So one Saturday 'e was passin' and wanted to impress 'er. So guess what 'e did. 'E didn't 'ave no chocolate or nothing like that to offer. 'E just starts talking loud to me and puttin' on the dog like, so she could 'ear what a nice boy 'e was.

BROOK: *(On top of the world.)* Come week after next Friday no more idlin' no more books, no teachers dirty looks.

CRAGGE picks up a book and kicks it across the room.

ADAMS: Head.

JORDAN: Saved.

BROOK kicks wildly, misses and falls down; they all laugh at him.

COLMAN: *(To JORDAN.)* Don't bloody push.

BROOK: Belt up.

CRAGGE: Goal.

ADAMS: *(Hugging CRAGGE.)* Beauty.

COLMAN: The cover's come off.

CRAGGE: Hide it in the desk.

BROOK: Another!

JORDAN: They'll start bloody missing 'em.

BROOK: *(Kicks the book against the wall, throwing up his hands and smiling.)* Score one like that tonight Craggsie, and the girls will love you.

ADAMS: *(On the lookout at the door.)* That new bloke's comin'.

Enter FREEMAN. Dead silence.

FREEMAN: What were you playing with?

ADAMS: Playin'?

FREEMAN: This book, wasn't it? *(He takes the ragged book off the floor.)*

ADAMS: *(Producing a football boot.)* This book, sir.

The boys laugh.

FREEMAN: Then I suppose there's no point in asking who did this.

JORDAN: We came in here and found it there.

BROOK: *(Insolently.)* That's the truth,

FREEMAN: *(Quietly to BROOK.)* What's your name?

BROOK: What's yours?

FREEMAN: *(Ignoring the insolence.)* Are there only five of you? What's happened to the rest of the class?

ADAMS: Gone down the drain.

The others often glance at BROOK for applause.

COLMAN: Left sir.

JORDAN: Left, left, right, left.

FREEMAN: Be quiet you.

ADAMS: The rest skidaddled the minute they touched fifteen.

COLMAN: We're leaving.

FREEMAN: So you leave when the term ends.

ADAMS: Tell us a little about yourself, sir.

JORDAN: *(A low grumble.)* What's 'appened to Barker?

ALL *except* CRAGGE: *(Led by BROOK.)* We want Barker, we want Barker!

FREEMAN: *(Gently.)* Quiet boys... I said quiet... Mr. Barker is away. I'll be teaching you for the next few days to the end of term.

COLMAN: A few days! There's the whole soggin' week.

FREEMAN: *(Gaining a laugh.)* Worse luck for me.

ADAMS: Brooksie won't stay the week, I bet.

BROOK: I never 'ave been 'ere a whole week, since I been to this school.

COLMAN: The worse lot in the school they've ever 'ad, they reckon us.

FREEMAN: *(To the leader, BROOK.)* Why don't you stay on in school?

Jeers and catcalls.

Doesn't your father want you to stay on and learn more?

The boys laugh.

VOICE: More!

BROOK: *(To them.)* Shut up. *(To FREEMAN.)* Wot's my dad got to do with it? It's my life.

FREEMAN: Doesn't anybody want to stay for the G.C.E.?

CRAGGE: 'Ands up who want to stay?

Everybody groans. No hands go up.

'Ands up.

No hands.

(To FREEMAN.) Bashful, ain't they?

COLMAN: No point in my stayin'.

JORDAN: 'E's got an apprenticeship.

COLMAN: My dad's in the print and 'e's getting me in.

FREEMAN: But you could stay on at school and learn. You don't have to be content with a trade.

JORDAN: I'm going into the docks, it's a skill and a privilege.

FREEMAN: Privilege?

JORDAN: I got two uncles in. You got to 'ave your family in the docks to get in.

FREEMAN: Don't any of you want to be educated?

CRAGGE: Look at you – you're educated and where did it get you – teaching!

ADAMS: What a life.

BROOK: You teach me to make dough and that's teaching.

FREEMAN: So money is all that counts?

ADAMS: *(Quite sincere.)* What else?

JORDAN: What's wrong with it?

FREEMAN: What's wrong with it!

COLMAN: *(Nasty, and resenting FREEMAN's attitude.)* You tell us, you're the teacher.

CRAGGE: Look at you. You've got G.C.E. and that. You'll be forty before you can buy a car without worrying. Look at you riding a pushbike and teaching.

ADAMS: What a life.

CRAGGE: Footballers drive a Cresta when they're twenty.

BROOK: *(Jeering at CRAGGE.)* He's gonna be one of them.

CRAGGE: *(To BROOK.)* Yeah, and we'll see who the crowd follow then. *(To FREEMAN.)* Look at Cliff Richard, Johnny Haynes, Helen Shapiro. D'you think they're educated. But they're the names ain't they. They make the news.

FREEMAN: What are you going to do?

CRAGGE: Who me?

FREEMAN: Yes, what job are you going into?

ADAMS: 'E asn't got a job. 'E'll be labourin'.

CRAGGE: I ain't much good with me 'ands.

FREEMAN: But you don't want to stay on at school.

BROOK: Get this thickie: they don't teach nothing that's any good to us.

FREEMAN: *(To CRAGGE.)* So what are you going to do?

COLMAN: Don't say we got no ambition.

BROOK: *(To COLMAN.)* I'll tell you what he's not going to do.

COLMAN: What?

BROOK: Helen! 'E tried to muck about and she insulted him…

CRAGGE: That's a lie.

FREEMAN: What's this?

ADAMS: So we want your name, sir, please, sir.

FREEMAN: Freeman, that's my name. What's your name?

ADAMS: Piggot. *(ADAMS is small.)* Lester Piggot.

FREEMAN: Now you'll understand that without knowing your names I can't control the class, so I'll punish anybody who trumps up a name. *(Suddenly pointing to ADAMS.)* You. What's your name?

ADAMS: Smith, sir.

FREEMAN: Alright. Let's take some current topic that interests you and talk about it. Any topic.

BROOK: Girls.

FREEMAN: Let's take the bomb, for instance.

JORDAN: Girls.

FREEMAN: I suggest the bomb. Let's hear what you think of…

COLMAN: Girls.

ADAMS: Girls.

BROOK: And ask old Cragge about 'Elen.

ALL: Girls! Girls!

FREEMAN: Don't shout at me please.

VOICES: We want girls.

FREEMAN: *(Taking up the challenge.)* Right then, girls. You then, talk about girls.

BROOK: 'Is name is 'Elen.

The boys laugh at CRAGGE.

FREEMAN: Start your talk.

CRAGGE: Well, I don't go much for the young talent because it ain't very well informed see?

Laughter.

I like 'em thirty, thirty-five, even forty like; get a bit a lolly and lot of fun out of 'em, see?

FREEMAN: *(Warningly.)* Good clean fun, eh, lad? Because that's what we're supposed to be talking about.

CRAGGE: But if you can't cop an amacher [amateur] like…

FREEMAN: Let's hear about the mixed youth clubs you lads go to.

CRAGGE: Not me. No youth for me. I told yer… Too easy… You dunno what you may catch.

BROOK: Easy wiv everyone except 'im.

ADAMS: *(To CRAGGE.)* As you was saying.

CRAGGE: *(To BROOK):* Helen's an easy feel but a hard lay if you really wanna know.

FREEMAN: *(Violently.)* Quiet!

COLMAN: You asked 'im, didn't you?

FREEMAN: *(To CRAGGE.)* Sit down.

CRAGGE: *(Very excited.)* If I can't find an amacher, I like the old pros, see, because you can…

Here follows a lewd gesture. Hell breaks loose. Enter HEADMASTER.

HEAD: Just stand where you are. I heard the noise. Could you just tell me what happened, Mr. Freeman?

FREEMAN: *(In a strained voice as though he is on trial.)* I said we'd take some subject and discuss it, say the bomb; and they said, 'no, girls'. So I thought I'd better not shy away from the subject. Then this boy said he liked the old pros best because you can – and made a filthy gesture.

HEAD: *(Aside to FREEMAN.)* Really these boys need special handling, Mr. Freeman, there's nothing much we can do! A few of them are on probation. *(Straightening his cane.)* Come here, Cragge. Filthy gestures, eh? Bend over!

CRAGGE obeys.

(To the whole class.) Girls… my mother was a girl. I have the deepest respect, indeed, reverence for her… My sister was

a girl too. *(To ADAMS, who is smiling.)* Yes, you worm, if your
filthy little mind would let you, you'd think of your mother
when you think of girls. I do… Now, I have from time to
time in my life, while I was going about my business, seen
women standing at street corners. I have assumed who
they were. But I have never in my life spoken to such a
woman. And certainly none of *my* sons have spoken to
such a woman. Neither have we ever spoken about them.
I do so for the very first time now and am very annoyed
indeed. *(To JORDAN.)* You muddy-minded clot over there,
you wouldn't understand… at any rate whatever you talk
about it in the streets or even in your own homes, we leave
the subject out of this school, right out. For let me tell you,
no man, no gentleman, ever talks about girls. *(To CRAGGE.)*
Bend over, boy.

*He whips CRAGGE who winces at the first stroke, and tries hard not
to wince for the other five.*

(After the whipping.) The subject Mr. Freeman suggested
you discuss was the bomb. You will stay in this classroom
after school tomorrow night and write me an essay on war.
It'll make you think. *(To CRAGGE.)* You've spent the last
two years doing nothing but playing, playing, playing and
talking, talking, talking. Just scraping into teams because
you're never steady. One match very good, another
hopeless.

ADAMS: *(Softly.)* It's better than playing nothing at all.

HEAD: What did you say?

ADAMS: I said is this gonna keep 'im off the side, sir.

HEAD: It won't if he's on it.

COLMAN: Won't 'e be in the team tonight, sir?

CRAGGE: *(Softly.)* I ain't worried.

HEAD: Cragge isn't worried. So long as people are talking about him he doesn't care if they're only saying he's a washout. He's easy to please.

BROOK: He ain't a killer.

HEAD: Nothing like it. Not even a threat. He's more like a false alarm. *(The pips go.)* You stay in during break, Cragge. The rest of you go.

Everyone goes out leaving CRAGGE. After a few moments COLMAN sneaks back to be with his mate, restored to favour by the caning.

CRAGGE: I'm going overseas. They pay your fare to Australia.

COLMAN: *(Unlike CRAGGE, he sticks to things.)* What about football?

CRAGGE: D'you think the head was hintin' that I ain't on the side?

COLMAN: Dunno.

CRAGGE: I suppose I won't go nowhere. I don't know what will 'appen. If I go into a job there'll be trouble. I won't like them fast as ever and you know what they'll be thinking of me.

COLMAN: You'll be a footballer. You might still be playing tonight.

CRAGGE: Don't know what I'll be. *(Anxious for a denial.)* Wasn't what he said a hint I was out?

COLMAN: You can always go into the factory your old man works at?

CRAGGE: Dunno, really. I done a turn there last summer 'olidays. Me 'and got tired carrying the bloody tea and I dropped the tray. And then another day I forgot the tea-break.

COLMAN: Didn't you 'ear the 'ooter?

CRAGGE: I 'eard it. Then I started thinkin' a something else. There was 'ell to pop. So there's one place that don't want me. My dad says word of this gets around and soon I'll 'ave to go over the water to find work... I been thinkin' of the R.A.F. but it was this Air Trainin' Course last weekend. Gave me the cramp that lot. Ten o'clock this duty, half past ten that, twelve o'clock the other. Bossed about by a little duck-arsed public school bloke I 'ated. God, I dream about that bloke's face and 'is blinkin' map-reading.

COLMAN: You couldn't be an officer with your accent.

CRAGGE: I could change easy, I know I could. *(Imitates.)* I do it all the time up West. I say to a bloke…

COLMAN: *(Mocking.)* Bloke!

CRAGGE: Gent.

COLMAN: Gent! It's man, you nut.

CRAGGE: Any'ow, I decided an officer, no matter 'ow 'igh 'e was, always obeyed some other bloke. You can't do much good of your own just obeyin' someone.

COLMAN: No, you can't.

CRAGGE: Don't you want to be something where you can do a bit of good?

COLMAN: I just want a big 'ouse where my granny can live without feelin' she ain't wanted.

CRAGGE: You'll 'ave that if you're doin' something big and good like Danny Blanchflower or Stan Matthews. Someone important.

COLMAN: A footballer ain't really important.

CRAGGE: The whole world knows you.

COLMAN: But 'e ain't doin' any good like.

CRAGGE: You don't know what you're sayin'! Sport brings nations together.

Silence.

COLMAN: Does the 'ead know the team for tonight, then?

CRAGGE: Dunno.

COLMAN: 'E must, mustn't 'e?

A long silence.

CRAGGE: You know what I sit 'ere thinking'. We could sell the metal ends of those desks and make a livin'.

COLMAN: They ain't worth a lot, them, though.

CRAGGE: If you sell a few every day you make enough to start a business when you leave school.

COLMAN: I ain't a thief.

CRAGGE: Well, do you think I am? Stealin' for something special ain't like bein' a thief. Stealing to start a business where you gotta work 'ard ain't like livin' off stealing. It in't the same thing.

COLMAN: If they nab you it's the same gaol.

CRAGGE: Probation. First offence.

COLMAN: Who would we flog 'em to?

CRAGGE: We can easy find out.

COLMAN: We can ask Brook.

CRAGGE: *We* can do this better than 'im. And we don't wanna let anyone else into this else there won't be any metal-ends left… It's a school, it won't miss 'em.

COLMAN: *(Tugging at a metal end.)* Means a lot to us, nothin' to them. We could get 'em off easy. Give me a hand – well come on!

CRAGGE: We mustn't use these. They know we've been in here.

COLMAN: But 'ere's this one nearly off already. You always dream up somethin', then when we're gonna *do* somethin' about it you ain't interested.

CRAGGE: They know we're in 'ere. We must get 'em off other desks.

COLMAN: When. *(Mocking him.)* Tomorrow or day after.

CRAGGE: We must find out first where we can flog 'em.

COLMAN: Couldn't we make a quid a day, do you think?

CRAGGE: Not these in 'ere any'ow.

COLMAN: 'Ow much for a shop?

CRAGGE: Dunno. Two hundred?

COLMAN: You're nuts! Thousands.

CRAGGE: About eight hundred

COLMAN: That's eight hundred days leaving out Saturdays and Sundays. That's two years. We'll be seventeen and still 'ere. You are a wet.

FREEMAN comes along the corridor and looks into the classroom.

FREEMAN: Get out of the building during break.

No answer from the boys.

What is it?

CRAGGE: You invited me to give on that subject.

FREEMAN: But not on that part of the subject.

CRAGGE: You didn't say no part. You just said girls. And then you nark to the headmaster.

FREEMAN: I said girls, not...

CRAGGE: Not what?

Enter BROOK.

FREEMAN: *(To the boys.)* Get out of the building during break. You know the rules.

BROOK: I wanna be indoors. Out there it's cold.

FREEMAN: Come on, Brook. Out!

BROOK: You send me to the 'eadmaster and 'e'll tell you 'e's tired of 'ittin' me.

COLMAN: It's time for the next period, anyway.

CRAGGE: What you've done ain't fair.

FREEMAN: All right, I've got that. You think it ain't fair.

BROOK: *(To CRAGGE.)* You think it ain't fair and 'e thinks it is. So what are you goin' to do about it. That's what 'e's askin' you.

FREEMAN: *(To BROOK.)* You make me sick! *(He turns to go.)*

CRAGGE: *(To FREEMAN's back.)* I'll do 'im tonight.

FREEMAN exits.

I'll do you tonight.

BROOK: 'E 'asn't 'eard you.

COLMAN: It ain't ever been done in the school yet, 'urtin' a master.

Pips go.

BROOK: *(Producing a knuckle-duster and offering it to CRAGGE.)* You can 'ave this knuckle-duster for a night for a tanner.

COLMAN: Blimey!

BROOK: Watch the door!

CRAGGE: *(Handing back the knuckle-duster.)* I don't want it.

BROOK: 'Ave it. What are you goin' to 'it 'im wiv, your breath, you dodger. 'Ave it and give me a tanner.

CRAGGE weakly throws him the sixpence and takes the knuckle-duster.

COLMAN: *(At door.)* Hey! Old Webster's coming. He's at the notice board, he's pinning up the team. The team for tonight.

Exit BROOK and COLMAN.
Enter WEBSTER. Re-enter BROOK.

BROOK: Reserve.

A long silence.

CRAGGE: *(Apprehensively.)* First?

BROOK: *(Going off gaily.)* Second.

CRAGGE smiles weakly. ADAMS and COLMAN re-enter.

BROOK: *(To ADAMS, exiting.)* Team's up.

CRAGGE: *(Mutters to ADAMS.)* I'm reserve.

ADAMS: First or second?

CRAGGE: Didn't even look.

WEBSTER: *(Concerned about CRAGGE not facing reality.)* What's the matter, Cragge boy, can't you read? When are you going to face up to things?

CRAGGE: A bloke 'ad me 'it this mornin' for nuffink.

JORDAN enters. WEBSTER starts his lesson.

WEBSTER: You sit down now and give me some attention… It's important to use the comma, or you'll never be able even to apply for a job.

ADAMS: Where' we're goin' you don't apply, you just get took.

Everybody laughs except CRAGGE.

WEBSTER: Write down the following sentences and punctuate them. 'The torch, symbol of learning, has been replaced by...' What is it, Cragge?

CRAGGE: Where's Brook?

ADAMS: *(Innocently.)* Ain't 'e 'ere?

CRAGGE: *(Challenging WEBSTER to do something about it.)* What's 'appened to 'im then?

WEBSTER: Gone for a stroll has he...? We'll see about that. I'll deal with him later... So when you have a short pause, it's a comma...

CRAGGE, in disgust, throws his exercise book loudly against the desk.

What's the matter?

CRAGGE: If I took a stroll you'd be sending the prefects after me.

WEBSTER: Just be quiet, lad.

CRAGGE: You blokes can't touch Brook, can you?

WEBSTER: I said, be quiet.

CRAGGE: You can't touch 'im though, can you?

WEBSTER: *(Gently.)* Go and stand outside.

CRAGGE: I just got in.

WEBSTER: You go outside. I'll tell you when to come in.

CRAGGE: The longer I stay 'ere the less I learn and that's a fact.

WEBSTER: You'll be glad you're leaving then.

CRAGGE: Big waste a time, this school. Look at the guys you see packin' a big bag a books regular to school. They 'ave no money to do nothin'. They don't know life. And don't know boozin'.

WEBSTER: Outside!

CRAGGE: They don't know Soho.

The class laughs, egging on CRAGGE.

WEBSTER: I said outside, boy.

CRAGGE: *(Standing his ground defiantly.)* They don't know twistin'.

More laughs.

They don't know gamblin' and swearin'.

WEBSTER: I said out!

ADAMS: *(Softly.)* Take 'im, Craggsie.

CRAGGE: There's gonna be trouble I tell you.

WEBSTER: *(Grabbing him.)* What trouble, eh, boy, what trouble?

CRAGGE: You take your greasers off me.

WEBSTER: *(Letting go.)* I'm sick and tired of the smell of violence in this school. All right, I started this last bit. Let's forget it these last few days, shall we?

ADAMS: *(Sotto voce.)* Ban the bomb!

CRAGGE: (*Sounding for the first time as unpleasant as BROOK.*) You lay off when I said, didn't you.

WEBSTER: Perhaps I shouldn't have, eh? Perhaps I shouldn't have. Now, outside!

CRAGGE is pushed.

Now, back to the comma. I am going to put a sentence on the blackboard and I want you to punctuate it for me. Take out your exercise books. Outside, Cragge.

CRAGGE: You four-kind son of a bitch. You crud.

Act Two

After school in the dark, CRAGGE is waiting. Enter FREEMAN with his bike from the bicycle shed, he discovers it has a flat tyre.

CRAGGE: It's flat. I let it down. Come on now. No headmaster to squeal to. They've all gone 'ome. You come on.

FREEMAN is frightened and dumb, only putting the bike between himself and CRAGGE.

You come on. *(CRAGGE whips out the knuckle-duster.)* Now come on.

FREEMAN: *(Breathing hard and scarcely able to speak he says meaninglessy.)* Shall I tell you... What on earth have you got there?

CRAGGE: Wot?

FREEMAN: You... Did you let down my tyre Cragge?

CRAGGE: Yeah, what about it?

FREEMAN: I suppose it's something that you admit it, and I suppose you could have slashed it and me be none the wiser.

CRAGGE: *(Sotto voce.)* Slash you... What about what 'appened to me this morning? Come on now, spit up about that. You 'ad me 'it this morning didn't you? I say the facts about girls and you have me hit.

FREEMAN: You weren't saying the facts about girls you were seeing how far you could go. Oh, put that thing away it's ridiculous!... All I can say is I didn't want you hit for what you said about girls but if I'd let you get away with it they'd have been throwing things at me next. You as well, because you want to cut a big figure.

CRAGGE: What do you mean cut a figure?

FREEMAN: Trying to impress the others.

CRAGGE: Showing off like?

FREEMAN: This morning Brook said let's talk about girls. So you had to go one better and say let's talk about tarts.

CRAGGE: I go one better every time but Brook's the leader.

FREEMAN: You conform to nothing, neither the gang nor the school and you get the dirty end of every stick.

CRAGGE: The gang and the school 'ave a bit in common, 'aven't they? The headmaster drives that luxury liner and 'as 'is own parking space. Brook loves that. And at staff meetings, all them teachers, two hundred blokes, shoot up when the headmaster comes in. Brook loves that again; and another thing: Brook says it's O.K. for the 'ead to be down on swearing 'cos if 'e wasn't 'e'd lose the manor...

FREEMAN: *(Interrupting.)* And anyway why bother to swear?

CRAGGE: 'Cos there's too many things make me puke. He'd lose the manor for us swearin' – but no matter how little we learn he don't lose nothing. For 'avin' most us leave 'ere content to borin' dirty work 'e gets the Mayor praisin' him. To hell with the lot of them anyway, I ain't content. That bloody 'eadmaster, 'e's imposin' 'imself on us. Toffs don't eat in the street so we mustn't. We ain't toffs that's why 'e can't teach us nothin'. Somethin' like that. We 'aven't learned nothin' any'ow and 'e's bloody paid to teach us... I dunno...

FREEMAN: Just a minute. You've got some sort of brain. Why've you never thought about staying on?

CRAGGE: I've stayed four years already and it's got me nowhere.

FREEMAN: It's better than pushing a barrow down Brixton.

CRAGGE: What about your bike?

FREEMAN: I'll go by bus. Take it to the school keeper – and take Miss Smith's as well... goodnight.

CRAGGE: *(Cheeky; of Miss Smith.)* Are you scratchin' 'er then?

FREEMAN: So what are you going to do when you leave?

CRAGGE: *(Caught off balance, forced to consider.)* Dunno. Get lost I expect.

FREEMAN: Are you on probation? *(No answer; seeing the others coming.)* You'll get jailed if you go on being lawless.

CRAGGE: You get jailed lawless or not, down 'ere.

FREEMAN: That's rubbish.

CRAGGE: That's life.

Exit FREEMAN. Enter Gang and Girls.

BROOK: 'And over me bruiser.

CRAGGE: Waste of a tanner, that was.

ADAMS: *(Looking at the knuckle-duster.)* Any blood?

HELEN: Let me 'ave a look.

ADAMS: It's a bloody knuckle-duster.

JORDAN: It ain't bloody, it's dry.

CRAGGE: *(Very defensive, fearing their reaction to what he has to tell.)* Waste of a tanner, I told you.

ADAMS: 'Ow long will 'e be in 'ospital?

BROOK: Why don't you dry up? *(To CRAGGE.)* What did you use?

SYLVIA: Did 'e scream?

BROOK: *(To SYLVIA.)* Look, if you don't shut your cake 'ole, I'll do you.

Roar of laughter.

HELEN: What did 'e say 'e'd used?

BROOK: 'E ain't 'ad a chance to say a thing yet. Will you dry up?

CRAGGE: You should 'ave 'eard 'im talking. Cor.

BROOK: So what did you do?

CRAGGE: Oh, he talked on and on. Begged hisself off.

COLMAN: Tried to talk 'imself out of it, did he?

BROOK: Let 'im tell it.

CRAGGE: That's all. 'E begged hisself off.

BROOK: 'E traps you into lettin' on about the birds then gets you caned for it. Then you let 'im smooth you over.

CRAGGE: I didn't.

ADAMS: Didn't you hit 'im wiv it *(i.e. knuckle duster.)*?

BROOK: *(Calmly.)* Let 'im tell.

CRAGGE: 'E apologized. Begged hisself off.

BROOK: So what you do when he done that.

ADAMS: They kissed goodnight.

BROOK: You fell on 'is bleedin' neck and cried.

CRAGGE: You couldn't a done no different. 'E as 'is judo belt, that master. Toss you a mile.

BROOK: Aw, you weeper. *(To the others.)* You comin'?

CRAGGE: Well, 'e apologised, 'e did an all. You ask 'im in the mornin'.

BROOK: *(Contemptuously.)* Ah, you go and ask 'im yourself.

BROOK goes off with the others following him. CRAGGE is left with bitter jealousy and a one-down feeling. Clutching for support he calls after one of the girls.

115

CRAGGE: Sylvia.

SYLVIA: *(Intensely embarrassed.)* Wot.

ADAMS: *(Derisively.)* You can 'ave 'er. *(Exit.)*

SYLVIA: *(Hostile.)* Wot was it you wanted?

CRAGGE: Knuckledusterin'. That's Brook's kinda work. 'E's just a thief with no brains. No brains 'e 'asn't. Now they're going into the caff eatin' what Brook buys 'em.

SYLVIA: No they're not, they're going to the graveyard.

CRAGGE: Wot?

SYLVIA: They want me an' 'Elen to go into graveyard wiv 'em. And I ain't going.

CRAGGE: *(Alarmed.)* 'Elen's goin' wiv them?

SYLVIA: You go and be wiv 'er.

CRAGGE: Let 'er go to bloody 'ell if she likes… All I know is there's always plainclothes coppers patrollin' that graveyard and they won't 'ave the nerve to go in.

SYLVIA: Brook seems to 'ave the nerve for anything.

CRAGGE: For takin' advantage.

SYLVIA: That's nerve as well.

CRAGGE: Getting people to do what they don't want to do.

SYLVIA: What d'you mean?

CRAGGE: I wouldn't be like him for anything.

SYLVIA: He's all right.

She is about to go.

CRAGGE: Can you ride a bike?

SYLVIA: Can I ride a bike!

CRAGGE: I learnt to ride underbar like this when I was that 'igh. *(The barbarian demonstrates on the flat tyre.)* No one taught me. Would you like a try?

SYLVIA: No.

CRAGGE: Come on, have a go.

SYLVIA: No.

CRAGGE: Come on.

She comes diffidently to the bike but her narrow skirt impedes her from climbing on with ease.

Ride on the cross-bar.

SYLVIA: Will you hold it for us?

He guides her round.

CRAGGE: If you 'ad one would you cycle all over?

SYLVIA: I don't ave one.

CRAGGE: You're too sheltered from life. You should be doin' things like cycling down to Brighton and 'aving a picnic off the road in the beautiful countryside, with food and a transistor, then on to the road again, racin' quite fast with the breeze in your face and your legs glowin'. But you never. D'you like goin' round with Brook and them?

SYLVIA: *(Sour grapes.)* I know I don't wanna get like 'Elen. Brook'll have her slippin' stuff out Woollies. Them shops, they're all eyes.

CRAGGE: 'E's a big mouth. 'E should be shouting paraffin for a living. Esso blue! *(He does the Esso Blue street cry. The 'E' becomes a long high 'A'.)* A's blue. *(He does it very well.)*

SYLVIA: *(Laughing.)* You ought to sell it, not 'im.

The unmeant irony wounds him and he shows it.

(Very friendly, soothing him.) I didn't mean nothin'.

CRAGGE: You won't do much wiv 'im except goin' to the pictures and wearin' eye-brow pencil, and 'angin' about wet-like, nattering.

SYLVIA: *(Friendly.)* Who is wet?

CRAGGE: You should be keepin' 'ealthy, cycling in the open this week-end, instead a coopin' up in the smog, your lungs gettin' yellow.

SYLVIA: I'm going out anyway, this week-end.

CRAGGE: Who with?

SYLVIA: 'Elen.

CRAGGE: *(Apprehensive.)* Just two of you.

SYLVIA: The gang was talkin' in the caff just now about something.

CRAGGE: What?

SYLVIA: *(Gently.)* I expect if they want you to know they'll tell you.

All silence. He's completely deflated.

CRAGGE: Didn't they say nothin' about tellin' me?

SYLVIA: No.

CRAGGE: It's some muckin' around wastin' time. They'll leave school and 'ave to troop into some dirty job for life. I've made up me mind… I'm gonna be doin' something – not just muckin' around.

SYLVIA: *(Not following.)* When are you talkin' about?

CRAGGE: I'm gonna be doin' the thing in life that takes the most nerve and makes the most money.

SYLVIA: I'm talkin' about this week-end.

CRAGGE: *(Not lifting his eyes.)* You could 'ave this bike *(Miss Smith's.)* For the week-end to cycle to Brighton.

SYLVIA: 'Ow could I?

For a second he can't get out an answer.

Whose is it then?

CRAGGE: I got another one (*FREEMAN's.*) as well. This is me cousin's and he don't want it clutterin' up the 'ouse. This week-end cycle down to Brighton with me.

SYLVIA: Me dad don't like me borrowin' things from people.

CRAGGE: Have it.

SYLVIA: No.

CRAGGE: What are you nervous about?

SYLVIA: I ain't.

CRAGGE: Then wheel the bloody thing away.

SYLVIA: I don't want a bike.

BROOK and HELEN re-enter.

Let's go with Brook this week-end, then another time…

CRAGGE: Yeah, you go wiv 'em then.

HELEN: *(Moving a little aside.)* Are you coming to the graveyard then, you and me and 'im and 'is friends.

SYLVIA: Not Jordan. Where is 'e?

HELEN: Soon be 'ere.

SYLVIA: I ain't goin'.

BROOK: *(To Sylvia; jeering.)* Then you're bloody on your own this week-end as well.

SYLVIA: *(Falling back on CRAGGE.)* I might be cyclin' down to Brighton wiv 'im.

BROOK: What on?

SYLVIA: *(Flaunting her independence of BROOK.)* 'Ow far is it to Brighton? I'll need a rain-cape and tent.

BROOK: I could get you a proper cape cut right for next to nothing.

SYLVIA: I'll buy me own cape.

BROOK: What you goin on?

SYLVIA: That bike.

BROOK: This bike?

CRAGGE: Yeah, I'm lending it to her.

BROOK: *(To CRAGGE.)* You're a wet drag *lending* it to 'er. You might as well sell it. You're gonna need a couple a quid in Brighton. Instead of lending it to 'er for the week-end, flog it to 'er for a bargain so you'll be flush.

HELEN: *(A born confederate.)* They're comin' in now ain't they, racin' bikes for girls.

SYLVIA: Are you sellin' it?

CRAGGE: And this shed as well.

BROOK: *(To SYLVIA.)* It's gonna be chromed to look new so one will see it's an old second-'and bike.

SYLVIA: If I was 'avin' it I'd 'ave it as it is.

BROOK: You can't be the girl with the black push-bike. You gotta be the flyer on the chrome.

CRAGGE: You're sellin' it then.

BROOK: Everyone sees I'm sellin' it. For ten quid. Chromed.

SYLVIA: But it's 'is bike.

BROOK: *(Moving CRAGGE away from the girls.)* Lendin' or sellin' it's larceny you timid nit... I reckon we could make a tenner a day on jobs like this.

CRAGGE: Freeman knows 'e left me 'ere wiv the bikes.

BROOK: Are ya chicken then? Are ya?

CRAGGE: You run your risks, I'll run mine.

BROOK: Ten quid for ten minute's work. Quid a minute.
That's wages. You'll go for life Whitbread like your Dad
and they'll retire you wiv a ribbon and a bundle of grass.

CRAGGE: If you're as barmy as you are I'll do me own
pinchin'.

BROOK: Whitbread's load'll be as safe with you as with a
bloody carthorse.

CRAGGE: You can say anything you like. I'd be a sittin' duck
for cops wiv that bike and you know it.

BROOK: If they found out. Any job's a risk.

CRAGGE: I'll choose me own risks.

BROOK: Any risk'll be too big for the likes a you. Any risk. *(To
the girls.)* You comin'?

*He jumps on FREEMAN's bike and coasts over to JORDAN, COLMAN
and ADAMS as they re-enter.*

SYLVIA: Is this the lot of 'em?

HELEN: There can't be no pairin' off, Brooksie says. 'E says 'e
wants 'is mates in as well.

SYLVIA: Just you wiv all them.

HELEN: And you.

SYLVIA: Tell 'em I ain't goin'.

HELEN: It's Brooksie wants you in.

SYLVIA: I wouldn't mind 'im. But not that lot. Let's just
wander away.

HELEN: You won't get far.

SYLVIA gets out of the way of JORDAN who brushes against her, then the boys talk among themselves.

COLMAN: Bloody one and six they are.

BROOK: *(Taking a look.)* I think it's old stock as well.

JORDAN: *(Referring to ADAMS and COLMAN.)* At the shop they was just gigglin' and wouldn't ask for nutten. *(To BROOK about ADAMS.)* 'E still ain't got one.

ADAMS: I didn't 'ave one and six.

COLMAN: 'E ain't comin. 'E's afraid somethin' will 'appen.

BROOK: 'E's another one.

ADAMS: 'Ow am I another one?

COLMAN: 'E means another one like Cragge.

CRAGGE: *(Holding his own.)* Everything's Cragge, you damn cretin. Me like 'im? I'll kick your bloody teeth in.

ADAMS: I feel somethin' will 'appen and I'm sayin' it.

BROOK: What will?

ADAMS: We'll be 'ad up for somethin' indecent and that's remand 'ome and I'm not goin' to one a them places.

BROOK: Shout so she bloody hears.

JORDAN: *(To ADAMS.)* Are you goin'?

ADAMS: Only if everyone else is.

JORDAN: *(To ADAMS.)* If. An iffin' bastard. *(To CRAGGE.)* You comin'?

BROOK: Leave him.

CRAGGE: She's not going with you, you know. Every girl ain't Helen.

COLMAN: Which one are we going to have then?

BROOK: Both of them. *(To the girls.)* We're goin'.

HELEN: *(To BROOK.)* Just a moment. *(To SYLVIA.)* Who don't ya fancy then?

SYLVIA: I don't even know 'em, except 'im. *(i.e. BROOK.)*

HELEN: *(To BROOK.)* She wants you a minute.

SYLVIA: Did I say that?

BROOK: What about the lark in the graveyard then?

SYLVIA: I'll go wiv you and 'Elen, if you want to. Not them.

BROOK: What's the good a that?

SYLVIA: Go with 'er, then.

BROOK: I'm not gonna be 'ere arguin'… Are you gonna be around wiv us?

SYLVIA: If you like.

BROOK: Come on, then.

SYLVIA: Not with them.

BROOK: You'd go wiv me, wouldn't you?

SYLVIA: I'd go wiv you and 'Elen.

BROOK: That's what I said. Well, if you go with me, you go with them. It's the gang of us.

HELEN: They could easily force you if they liked.

SYLVIA: I'd tell me mum.

BROOK: Bleedin' tell-tit. I knew it. Tell-tale tit.

HELEN: She wouldn't tell.

BROOK: *(In a nasty voice.)* Come on.

SYLVIA is too much on the verge of tears to say anything.

CRAGGE: Who 'e can't buy 'e bashes.

ADAMS: More power to 'im.

SYLVIA: *(To BROOK.)* I'll go wiv you any day.

BROOK: *(Sweet reason.)* Just do what I tell you and they'll do whatever I tell 'em to.

SYLVIA: What will you tell 'em?

BROOK: Let's go.

SYLVIA: *(Weeping.)* Brooksie, what will you tell 'em?

BROOK: I'll tell 'em to leave off if you don't want.

SYLVIA: What am I goin' wiv 'em for, then?

BROOK: Don't argue... Are you?

SYLVIA: No.

BROOK: I could force you. Like to bet?

SYLVIA: I don't want you to force me.

BROOK: So what are we on then?

CRAGGE intervenes and taking BROOK aside says very anxiously.

CRAGGE: If you force 'er and she goes 'ome bawlin' and 'er dad goes to the police you'll be 'ad up and she'll tell about you tryin' to flog 'er the bike. So go wiv 'Elen and leave her.

BROOK: I'll 'ave 'er in.

ADAMS: She ain't goin'.

JORDAN: We've missed 'er.

CRAGGE: *(Sardonic.)* 'E'll 'ave 'er there and on 'er back in no time.

COLMAN: *(Throws up a ball and tries to catch it in his mouth.)* Missed it. God doon it.

ADAMS: *(Sings.)* There's a hole in my Liza,
Dear bucket, dear bucket…

BROOK: Shut up.

ADAMS: Why?

BROOK: *(Power.)* 'Cos I says.

ADAMS: *(Serious protest.)* It's five of us against just 'er.

CRAGGE: *(Not to be included.)* Four.

ADAMS: Four to one.

BROOK: That's the fun, fool.

ADAMS: The grass in the graveyard's wet.

JORDAN: We'll 'ave 'em between the grass and us. *(To COLMAN.)* Throw it up again. *(To the girls.)* Bet 'e muffs.

HELEN: Bet 'e doesn't.

SYLVIA: I say 'e muffs. No, I say 'e doesn't.

COLMAN muffs.

ADAMS: I told you.

JORDAN: *(To SYLVIA.)* Catch.

He hurls the ball brutally at her back but misses. She doesn't see.

CRAGGE: *(Shocked; dry.)* I'm goin' 'ome to wash me dog.

BROOK: *(Urgently, to CRAGGE.)* 'Ang on.

ADAMS: What's gonna be 'appennin' 'ere, then?

JORDAN: *(Brutally sadistic.)* We gonna… We gonna… We gonna…

COLMAN: *(Laughs.)* Sh-h-h.

JORDAN: *(Sadistically sexy.)* Machine-gun 'em.

BROOK: *(Cold.)* If they die from overwork we can bury 'em right there and then.

SYLVIA has been bouncing the ball and it goes to BROOK who pockets it.

(Friendly.) So let's go,

SYLVIA: Give it to us.

BROOK: Go to 'ell.

HELEN: *(Soft voice, to SYLVIA.)* Now you've 'ad it.

SYLVIA: I don't care. I said I'd go wiv you and 'im.

BROOK: *(To SYLVIA.)* How long are we gonna be standin' 'ere, then?

SYLVIA: Till I make up my own mind.

BROOK: What do you 'ave against me mates?

SYLVIA: *(Pointing to JORDAN.)* Look at 'im. Rag bag, that one.

BROOK: That's only one.

SYLVIA: Do we count 'im out, then?

BROOK: 'E's still my mate so 'e's gotta be yours.

SYLVIA: Only if I 'ave 'im.

BROOK: Make up your mind.

SYLVIA: I am doin'. Can't you just wait?

BROOK: Not much longer.

SYLVIA: Don't then.

BROOK: If we leave 'im out for the present what about the others?

SYLVIA: What about 'em?

BROOK: Are you takin' the mickey out a me then?

SYLVIA: I ain't. I'm sorry.

CRAGGE: *(To HELEN.)* Can't you go wivout 'er?

HELEN: She's makin' up 'er mind.

BROOK: *(Wilful; of SYLVIA)* She's got to come.

CRAGGE: She doesn't want to. She's only a teaser.

BROOK: *(Brutally.)* She's comin'. *(To SYLVIA, turning on a more moderate voice.)* Do it my way today and tomorrow your way.

HELEN: Just this once.

BROOK: Yeah.

SYLVIA: Can't we not bother. Let's not go at all.

BROOK: Well then you can bloody well not 'ang around me.

SYLVIA: But I like being with you, Brooksie.

BROOK: Well?

SYLVIA: The caff I liked.

BROOK: You've gotta do other things, 'aven't you, wot other people like.

SYLVIA: Does every girl 'ave to then?

BROOK: Sometime.

A long silence.

So are you comin'?

SYLVIA: All right.

BROOK is now very tender with SYLVIA.

Can't we go somewhere else than the bloody graveyard? All I know is there's always plainclothes passing through.

BROOK: Who told you about plainclothes?

SYLVIA: *(Pointing to CRAGGE.)* 'Im.

CRAGGE: I told her before but she's repeating it now 'cos she doesn't want to go.

BROOK: *(To SYLVIA.)* Do you want to go?

SYLVIA: If she is.

COLMAN: *(To CRAGGE.)* So who's a no gut? You!

ADAMS: Who's a no gut? You!

JORDAN: Who's a no gut?

HELEN: You!

ADAMS: *(Jeering at CRAGGE.)* She might go tell 'er dad.

COLMAN: You don't want to be in no trouble!

ADAMS: 'E thinks people won't love 'im.

HELEN: No one'll speak to him.

JORDAN: You'll go and nark won't ya!

SYLVIA: Narker!

ADAMS: Welsher!

COLMAN: Kick 'im!

CRAGGE: Try.

BROOK: I'm pushin' ya. *(Pushing him.)*

JORDAN: Look at him running.

CRAGGE: I've got to find a pump for the bike.

BROOK: Runnin'.

CRAGGE: Say anythin' you like.

COLMAN: 'E's bloody cryin'.

CRAGGE: *(Tears in his face and voice.)* You think I'm her you can do what you like with.

BROOK: All right then.

> *BROOK pushes then punches. All join in. There's a fight, and CRAGGE, taking fright, is wickedly beaten. He lies on the ground kicking; the others shout as they go off, their voices receding.*

BROOK: Whitbread cart-horse.

RECEDING VOICES: Whitbread cart-'orse. Whitbread cart-'orse.

ACT THREE

SCENE ONE

The classroom the following evening after school. The boys have been kept in to do their essay on war. FREEMAN sits reading.

ADAMS: Sir's been kept in wiv us.

COLMAN: Brooksie ain't turned up.

JORDAN: I notice that since Sylvia told 'er dad we done 'er Brook's keepin' scarce.

COLMAN: Can't blame 'im. 'Er dad's jealous.

FREEMAN: Come on, shut up and write. *(Impatient to get home.)* No one finished a page yet? You've been at it nearly an hour.

JORDAN: I bloody forget what we was kept in for.

COLMAN: If you hadn't blabbed about bloody tarts we wouldn't be here.

FREEMAN: Belt-up.

The scene slows down to a gentle sleepy murmur.

JORDAN: Nine days to go in this bloody prison.

ADAMS: One cell or another wot's the odds?

JORDAN: Wot you think 'er dad'll do?

COLMAN: Nothin'. Forget it. It'll blow over.

Silence.

ADAMS: Colley's done nearly half a page.

COLMAN: Good this is.

Silence.

ADAMS: Old Webster says, you must be vivid and put in commas.

COLMAN: 'Ow d'you spell total destruction. Write it down 'ere.

FREEMAN: *(To COLMAN.)* That's coming on. *(He picks up ADAM's essay and reads it out.)* 'If they called me up and I had the bomb to drop on a Russian town I'd think of it as London and instead of dropping a bomb on them I'd fly out to the mid-ocean with it, and sink it in the heart of the sea… and for that I'd get the sack and maybe they drop one on us, but so what, there is better jobs or if someone's going to be dead it might as well be us. That's how I argue but not my dad…'

CRAGGE: Your dad isn't a nut.

FREEMAN: It's very good. Carry on. Very good.

JORDAN: I couldn't think of nothing.

COLMAN: Come over 'ere and 'ave a look at mine.

FREEMAN: Good. *(Going over to CRAGGE.)* Three lines in nearly an hour.

CRAGGE: I'm thinkin' about a job.

ADAMS: *(Mocking.)* Professional footballer.

CRAGGE: *(Unable to cope.)* Be insultin'.

FREEMAN: Cut this out.

ADAMS: *(Expert baiting.)* You the stooge and Brook the guv. All your life.

FREEMAN: *(Severely.)* All right!

CRAGGE: *(To ADAMS.)* Rather than muck in wiv 'em like you did, lemme die.

ADAMS: You don't die. Nothin' like that. You stay alive watchin' Brook live it up.

CRAGGE: Yeah and dodgin' cops.

COLMAN: If Sylvia goes to the law, she'll tell 'em you tried to give 'er a bike.

CRAGGE: That's peanuts. That ain't rape.

JORDAN: Rape? She was willin'.

ADAMS: That ain't wot she's sayin' now. She's saying we broke and entered.

COLMAN: There was nothin' to break Brooksie said, and he was there wasn't he, living the life.

CRAGGE: He'll live it up in a cell.

JORDAN: No one's in for ever.

CRAGGE: *(Scornful; passionate.)* No, it ain't forever. He comes out but 'e's a bit behind and 'e'll wanna be laughin'. So 'e'll thieve, and blow the tickle like it ain't 'is, then thieve and thieve again till 'e's copped and bangled; in and out of a horse box; his name bawled out to come and stand before a man like himself. Two years; three; which-ever the man happens to think.

JORDAN: All right. So 'e does 'is bird like a gent.

CRAGGE: Yeah. And 'e's well-liked in there same as out 'ere, the reg'lar guy, he is; cons want to share his bed. Lemme finish. He's a criminal then. Soon 'e spends 'arf his life doin' time, a failin' old geezer. The way the cops are gettin' to 'ave 'im on their 'ands' sorta pathetic. In the end he's a rotten shambles, crawlin' 'ome to nick. That's Brook.

ADAMS: 'E's getting' 'ard.

CRAGGE: You're a huddler. You'll always end up muckin' in with them and I won't and they can tell. So I get beat up. But you'll get pipped, you lot. I'll do better in life than a bunch of bastards warming round Brook.

COLMAN: Wot a sad load a dreams, this geezer.

FREEMAN: *(Trying to break this up; to JORDAN.)* You go and see if Mr. Webster's still here.

JORDAN: What for?

FREEMAN: I wanted a lift home on his motor-bike. Satisfied?

JORDAN exits.

O.K. boys, take it home and finish it. You make sure you finish that. About another page. And if it's good all the way through we'll send it to the school newspaper.

ADAMS: You ain't serious.

FREEMAN: O.K. Buzz.

ADAMS: *(Walking to the door, clowning.)* 'E'll put me in the newspaper chaps. Adams in print. The only print I'll ever be in is fingerprint.

FREEMAN: Oh God, can't you just stop talking and think?

ADAMS: Such an undertakin'.

COLMAN: Ain't you gonna wish us lots a lolly out in the world. You ain't gonna see much of us again.

ADAMS: Wish us all we wish ourselves. It ain't very much.

COLMAN: 'E won't.

ADAMS: Well, good night, cock.

FREEMAN: *(Of ADAMS and COLMAN.)* Fools. Probably leaving school to run telegrams.

CRAGGE: Not Colman. Colman's a politician. 'E just kept watch in the graveyard, so he's clean if the law starts askin'.

FREEMAN: Were you in with 'em?

CRAGGE: No, I'm clean. No worries, ever again. Not me. I remember me uncle comin' home from prison and sayin' 'I'm here again.' Loud. It's a family thing. But not me. I'm gonna be somethin'.

FREEMAN: You'll do better with your brains than at football. Why didn't you write anything just now?

CRAGGE: You call Adams's simple guff writing. He's gonna be droppin' his bomb in the ocean, a guy who runs with the crowd. What about that contradiction. Why don't that come into his essay.

FREEMAN: That's fair criticism.

CRAGGE: *(With great force and bitterness.)* Yet the newspaper's open to him. The first time the bloody newspaper's offered to our lot it's to him.

FREEMAN: You alone know how good a writer you are if you write nothing. He wrote a page.

CRAGGE: Quality?

FREEMAN: The best in the class. You're incredible the way you hate others' success. I believe you hate even your own, and defeat yourself: up against it with your mates just now, instead of producing a better essay than Adams's you write three lines.

CRAGGE: I was thinking about me dad.

FREEMAN: What does he do?

Silence.

CRAGGE: *(Wearily.)* 'E works… Once upon a time, 'e 'ad a business. Then 'is business bust. Then T.B. One man. 'E was 'opin' for a break and that's wot 'e got. The back a me 'ead tells me nothin' in the world can be right when that can happen.

FREEMAN: It wouldn't be his fault that he failed.

CRAGGE: His fault? His luck. Me dad's been a fair stooge all 'is life but I ain't gonna be. Sometimes I believe I can do anything. But I can't decide wot. It's me whole life so it's gotta be somethin' good to 'elp stop war and that. I was for war in the argument just now wasn't I? *(Vain even in vice.)* Bet you didn't notice that? Did you? In an argument whatever it's about I just say the opposite to win. I argue about which trumpeter is better than which without 'aving 'eard neither a them. It shows I don't wanna be good, just big, like Brook and this bloody 'eadmaster, and I think about that, even in my sleep I think about it and wake up with me mind aching. And it's also the decision of givin' your whole life to a think. The other day I sweat deciding to give up for life the things I'd 'ave to give up to be a real Christian, like. I decided, then the next day changed me mind, then decided, then changed me mind again. Instead I was gonna be a rock and roll singer and give concerts in Moscow. Then I decided to be a footballer and 'ere I am now.

FREEMAN: Would writing up sports for the newspaper interest you?

CRAGGE: How?

FREEMAN: You could report on football matches.

CRAGGE: Me?

FREEMAN: Yes.

CRAGGE: *(Immediately taken but disliking to appear so.)* I won't be 'ere much longer.

FREEMAN: Do you want to or don't you?

CRAGGE: I ain't particular. If Adams could be in it it don't mean nutten. You can't praise me if you praise 'im.

FREEMAN: You don't want to.

CRAGGE: *(Pauses.)* I don't mind. But if I go to a sixth-form bloke like, and give them a report they won't want me 'aving nothin' to do with it. They mightn't do nothin' about it.

FREEMAN: You report the match. Hand it in. If it's good they'll use it.

CRAGGE: They wouldn't 'ave nutten to do wiv me, except 'ave a laugh. Take the mick.

FREEMAN: If it's any good I'll get it in to Mr. Webster.

CRAGGE: Will it be good though?

FREEMAN: That's up to you.

CRAGGE: *(Eagerly.)* There's a house match goin' on in the park now. How about that? I'll write it up and you pass it in to old Webster. O.K.?

FREEMAN: Fine.

CRAGGE: Swear to God.

FREEMAN nods. WEBSTER comes in.

WEBSTER: Any trouble Mr. Freeman?

CRAGGE: *(To FREEMAN.)* You ask 'im now.

FREEMAN: Could we get a report on tonight's match into the newspaper? He's going to write the report.

WEBSTER: *(Not showing his doubts.)* Cragge putting pen to paper. Very good. I'm not editing any longer but I'm sure it'll be all right.

CRAGGE races out.

They don't know thank you. Have you been threatened yet?

FREEMAN: Yes.

WEBSTER: At least we build up their muscles. Gym and football and free milk.

FREEMAN: Cragge wants success but has a deep grudge against it because people he loves didn't have it. His father had loads of trouble so defeats himself in sympathy and hates the people who go around succeeding.

WEBSTER: I've enough on my plate without psychology.

FREEMAN: How good is he?

WEBSTER: Who'll ever know. He never does enough work. No practice, so even what he does do is erratic. He'll probably write as well as he played football and come next week Friday, thank God, he'll be rid of us, bound for the *Mirror*.

FREEMAN: He talks, but he talks well.

WEBSTER: Cockney patter. No depth to it. You wanted a lift?

SCENE TWO

The classroom. CRAGGE is at his desk writing. The pips go for the end of break.

Enter COLMAN, JORDAN, ADAMS and BROOK. JORDAN just sits worried and mostly silent.

BROOK: Why do they keep blokes 'ere till they're fifteen?

ADAMS: 'Cos fifteen's the age of puberty.

CRAGGE: How d'you spell unleashed?

COLMAN: What for?

CRAGGE: I'm writing up last night's match for the newspaper.

ADAMS: Freeman wanted me to do the write up and I turned 'im down.

CRAGGE: And I'm doin' it.

JORDAN: What's puberty?

ADAMS: When your balls drop and you can give 'er pups. That's part of the trouble we're in. They might be breedin'.

BROOK: *(Of JORDAN.)* 'E's worried stiff. If stiff's the word.

CRAGGE: How do you spell unleashed? 'The Arnold House boys unleashed an attack…'

COLMAN: I pass.

137

BROOK: Nick yourself a dictionary from London County Council.

ADAMS: Do you know what a bloke told me last Saturday when he offered me two pounds fifteen a week to work in 'is firm as a tea-boy. 'E said 'I started on five bob, I did. When I went out into the world I started at the princely sum of five shillings a fortnight.'

COLMAN: What did you tell 'im?

ADAMS: I said that was nineteen hundred.

CRAGGE searches through the Mirror.

CRAGGE: Where's bloody unleashed?

COLMAN: Write it down 'ow you think and let old Freeman correct it. It's what he's paid for.

CRAGGE: Got it.

ADAMS: Tea-boy. You might as well pittle and play with the steam. I ain't gonna be no tea-boy, van-boy, nuffink like that.

COLMAN: *(A bit smugly.)* Someone's gotta do the dirty work.

ADAMS: Crawlin' about a bleedin' office, runnin' everybody's errands. You don't wanna be that.

CRAGGE: I'll head it 'Drama in the Park'.

JORDAN: Sounds like a bloke interferin' with little boys... The 'ead's comin'. Wot for?

COLMAN: Nothin'. Ain't you got the wind up.

BROOK: He's gonna be fatherly about somethin'. Or teach us manners. He tries 'ard, the old nit.

Enter HEADMASTER and FREEMAN.

HEAD: Put on your ties the lot of you.

ADAMS: We lost 'em, sir, and we're leavin' so it ain't any use buyin' any.

JORDAN: And inside we won't need 'em.

HEAD: When did you lose them?

ADAMS: Just last night, sir. We left them all together in the gym, and when we came back they was lost.

JORDAN: Someone must a nicked the lot.

HEAD: Mr. Freeman, please fix them up with ties from the lost property.

FREEMAN exits obediently.

I want to bring to your notice the arrangements for prize-giving. When and if you come tomorrow night, and I trust many of you, appropriately dressed, will avail yourselves of something a little different, you will report to Mr. Freeman and he will show you where to sit. I know there are none of you getting prizes but there's no reason why you shouldn't come and give those who are support. You boys haven't always contributed as much as you should in your years at school. And I hope you will make one last effort at the prize-giving tomorrow and contribute your presence. School uniform, please, ties, caps, and your best behaviour. I'm sure it will be a worthwhile occasion and you'll all benefit. Any further instructions will be announced over the tannoy. Now I'll just read over the list of boys who are leaving. *(Pause.)* All of you, in fact, is that right?

JORDAN: What's the use a staying. They don't learn you to talk no better and that's what gives you the better jobs.

HEAD: That, or settling down to work for G.C.E.

CRAGGE: 'Ow can we know till we've left whether we're leaving, Sir?

CRAGGE's mates would be hostile if they knew he was now uncertain about leaving, so he has to appear merely to be pulling the HEADMASTER's leg.

HEAD: Don't follow.

CRAGGE: Well, I mean unless you 'ave a good job to go to, Sir.

HEAD: Still don't follow.

CRAGGE: 'Cos you might change your mind when it comes to it, about diggin' the road or window cleanin' up there sixty feet above the ground floor in the depths a winter. You might decide school's less exertin' and a bit warmer like and you'd rather be an 'eadmaster.

The boys laugh at the HEAD.

HEAD: Have you changed your mind then, Cragge?

CRAGGE: But supposin' I want to by next Friday. Why do we 'ave to be pushed out on Wednesday evening?

HEAD: Against Cragge I will put uncertain... Thank you.

CRAGGE: Uncertain as Friday comin', that's me. *(This is for the boys' benefit.)*

The pips go for the end of school.

ADAMS: Can we go now, guv?

HEAD: Yes, go. Good night.

He exits and all the boys except CRAGGE and BROOK.

BROOK: Comin'? *(He's trying to get CRAGGE back into the gang.)*

CRAGGE: I can't. I gotta stop 'ere.

FREEMAN re-enters with a load of ties.

BROOK: *(To CRAGGE.)* See you. *(To FREEMAN, politely.)* Here's another. *(He pulls his school tie from his back pocket and adds it to the lot. Exit BROOK.)*

CRAGGE: I stopped in 'ere all break, choppin' and changin'
me report on the match.

FREEMAN: Nil desperandum.

CRAGGE: What's that?

FREEMAN: What does it sound like?

CRAGGE: Dunno.

FREEMAN: Can I see it?

*FREEMAN reads it. CRAGGE watches him anxiously. FREEMAN
smiles once or twice. CRAGGE fidgets. Enter WEBSTER.*

WEBSTER: *(Coming and looking over FREEMAN's shoulder.)* What's
this? Cragge's report! 'Headed and missed' spelt m-i-s-t.

FREEMAN: *(To CRAGGE.)* You can leave me this.

*CRAGGE starts to walk away before anything can happen to spoil
the reception.*

CRAGGE: Is that O.K., then?

FREEMAN: It's fine.

CRAGGE: I mean, will they 'ave it in the newspaper and all
that?

FREEMAN: Yes, it's good.

CRAGGE: But will they 'ave it in?

WEBSTER: They try to, if it's any good.

CRAGGE exits, anxious, hopeful.

FREEMAN: *(Wearily.)* Why does it have to take me the best
part of half a day to get this report into the newspaper?
And I'm still not certain if it's got in. No wonder boys
are left stranded if everything takes so much trouble. The
school's too big, you have to go through so many people.

WEBSTER: *(Interested in CRAGGE's work.)* 'The most talked about match for the season will be the one last night between Stevenson and Arnold House. Arnold's snappy forwards, from the whistle, unleashed a ripping attack on the Stevenson defence which were doing a good job, marking their men and fighting back.'

Does it bear any relation to the match, or did he copy it from a newspaper? I suppose he copied the clichés, but that's all right for a start. Nothing wrong with that. And the boys will enjoy reading it. But after next Friday he'll have forgotten all this.

FREEMAN: Whether he leaves or not next Friday, this makes him know he can do something besides fooling. But I think now he'll stay.

WEBSTER: *(Nicely.)* Like to bet?

SCENE THREE

Next evening after school. CRAGGE is at the window looking at the preparations for prize-giving.

CRAGGE: Cups and books for the prize-giving tonight. How many bloody cups they taking in? Don't them sixth-form blokes love carrying them?

JORDAN: Drop 'em! *(He's very nervy.)*

CRAGGE: They been shining them all day.

JORDAN: It's all right if you're getting a prize like but they ain't giving me no prize… Who's dealing me another fag? You don't get 'em where I'm goin'.

CRAGGE: What's up?

JORDAN: The heat's on.

CRAGGE: When?

JORDAN: The law's on to 'Elen. They want her to say we
threatened Sylvia… It ain't probation second offence.

CRAGGE: Brook will stop her leakin'. It's his line, wimmen.
Line is line. You gotta find your own line.

JORDAN: Wot's mine… Doin' time… It's misery in the nick
with the likes a Brook. You either knuckle under or peg out
or spend your life defendin' yourself. *(Of CRAGGE.)* You're
in the clear. But you ain't never in the clear down 'ere. It's
the gang of us. Didn't your family tell you?

CRAGGE: I'm stayin' on 'ere. I can do better with my brains
than with me feet, I know that. I can always see things that
need arguin' and find the argument: that's brain. And it
comes to me like birds come to Brook.

JORDAN: Give me the birds.

CRAGGE: That's barmy. I wanted football and rock 'n' roll.
But only because when you're born down here and think
you're goin' to be big you go after the big things you know
about, like rock 'n' roll and football; even fiddlin'. Then
you find you're only comin' second in them all the time,
but there's nothing else except birds and you're no good
with them. I played football like a natural only sometimes,
and dreamed it only now and then. But I always dream up
arguments.

Enter ADAMS.

ADAMS: Brook's bringin' 'Elen up 'ere. 'E's keeping her happy.

JORDAN: She can't come in 'ere. She ain't even a nice girl.
The 'ead would 'ave a fit. And there's staff around.

ADAMS: She'll have them whistling.

CRAGGE: She'll 'ave Brook whistling any tune she likes to
keep 'er sweet.

ADAMS: He's got to bring her in. He has a bet on with Colley.

JORDAN: Big deal.

CRAGGE: There's hundreds of cleaners around doing up the place for prize-giving, so bringing Helen up here's nothing.

JORDAN: She's too young to pass for a bloody cleaner.

ADAMS: He'll never get by all them busy bastards up and down them stairs.

CRAGGE: Oh they can't see for looking this lot. The headmaster'll pass this tarty cleaner coming along the corridor and he'll wonder, then he'll look back and see her bum swinging like a pail and think yeah, that's all right, that's a cleaner.

Enter HELEN.

HELEN: He won!

Enter BROOK and COLMAN.

COLMAN: Blimey.

HELEN: You won, you won.

CRAGGE: There's hundreds of cleaners about.

COLMAN: This wasn't the bet.

BROOK: I brought her up.

COLMAN: There's hundreds of visitors 'cos it's prize-giving. It's no bet on a day like this.

BROOK: Pay me.

COLMAN: Who won, Craggsie?

CRAGGE: All I wanna know is, does it rate an article in the bloody newspaper?

COLMAN: I could bring her up on a day like this. Lay a bet.

HELEN: I feel safer with him. What a glass-house! People can see everything you do. I feel eyes all over. Where do you sit?

BROOK: On me arse… Why can't they have a mirror on the wall so a person can see theirselves.

HELEN: What's he dressing up for?

BROOK: The prize-giving.

JORDAN: Yeah, let's dress him up for the prize-giving.

HELEN: He ought to have a collar.

JORDAN: Anybody got a collar?

HELEN: He can't wear them drainpipes either.

COLMAN: He needs a pair of pants.

JORDAN: He can't sing the bleeding hymn in drainpipes.

ADAMS: *(To HELEN.)* You lend him a pair of pants, go on, lend him a pair of pants.

COLMAN: He's got to represent us lot.

JORDAN: He's got to sit in the great hall and put out his fag.

COLMAN: So he can go up and shake the old people's hands.

ADAMS: Well done! Well done! Old grey balls.

JORDAN: My lords ladies and gentlemen…

COLMAN: Me lord stiff!

ADAMS: Me lord 'elpless!

BROOK: Me lord 'elpless and lady never-had-a-gent.

JORDAN: My lord Jo
Have a go.

JORDAN *and* COLMAN: Have a go with lady Flo!

ALL *except* CRAGGE: My lord Jo
Have a go
Have a go with lady Flo!

BROOK: Let's go to the prize-giving and help the headmaster out with a few remarks.

COLMAN: There's a few things I could tell him.

BROOK: Let's boo him.

JORDAN: *(Not believing he'll do it.)* Garn!

BROOK: Let's boo him.

ADAMS: Boo him.

COLMAN *and* JORDAN: Boo him.

BROOK: Yeah let's break the joint up.

JORDAN: Yeah!

ADAMS: Yeah!

COLMAN: Yeah!

HELEN: Can I come too?

BROOK: *(To CRAGGE.)* What about it?

CRAGGE: Who wants to hang around them?

BROOK: You do. You'd rather lick up to him 'cos you need a paper. *(To the others.)* Let's boo him.

VOICES: Boo, boo, boo.

BROOK: We'll give them something to remember us.

ALL: *(Going)* Boo! Boo!

CRAGGE silent and anxious, watches them run off.

SCENE FOUR

We fade into the prize-giving. The HEADMASTER speaks to the audience.

HEAD: My Lord Bishop, Mr. Mayor, Lady Gibson, Members of the Board of Governors, ladies and gentlemen: we are really most honoured in having such a distinguished list of guests with us here tonight. I particularly want to express my gratitude to the Mayor and Lady Gibson. Lady Gibson is, of course, no stranger to us, and a living example to the boys of dignity, simplicity and charm. I welcome our guests especially as I am able to report, frankly, a proud year to add to our record. The things this school stands for, not only three Rs, but integrity, and character, we have, I hope, continued to cherish. Our aim in a comprehensive school of this size is not success in any grand worldly sense. We must face the fact that the dream of many of our boys here is to get into the trades and factories as quickly as possible and earn high wages. Well, good. I don't condemn that. On the contrary, I am often grateful that they have escaped what seems to me the ruling passion in our world – I mean the uneasy ambition to hustle one's way to notoriety and wealth. In an age when we are eaten up with a curiously unsatisfying acquisitiveness is it not time a voice in the wilderness called attention to our older English traditions of content. But whether our lads end up in the trades or in one of your factories, Mr. Mayor, I want them to leave here with a dawning awareness of the finer things of life – music, art, literature and that forgotten solace, nature. And the task of awakening them to these abiding values down here is frankly a man-size job. You can perhaps have little idea how much sacrifice on the part of all concerned: staff, and parents and boys...

Boo.

... is involved in the running of a school of this size.

Boo, boo.

147

I was saying that some of you might have little idea how much sacrifice…

Boo, boo, boo.

Those would not be my boys.

Boo, boo, boo.

You see the sort of thing we have to put up with in this area, will someone catch the ruffians and have them removed. – You see, that's the sort of thing…

Boo, boo.

… that gives you a vivid idea

Boo, boo.

SCENE FIVE

The classroom the next day. CRAGGE alone reading the school newspaper.

Enter COLMAN, BROOK, ADAMS.

COLMAN: They ain't done your stuff.

ADAMS: 'E won't tell no lies no more, no more, no more, no more… Jordan's findin' out if it's the booing he's talkin' to them six-formers about.

COLMAN: 'E'll sweat dreamin' about those boos.

BROOK: *(Friendly to CRAGGE.)* You should a come. 'E just spluttered out. All wind and piss like a barber's cat. 'E's a back-rubbin' bum. We should a kicked 'im and the distinguished guests.

COLMAN: *(Nastily.)* Leave it to your mates.

CRAGGE: *(Gently.)* It's alright, isn't it, booin' 'im for bein' a back-slapper so you get backslapped by all the people you tell.

COLMAN: *(Nasty.)* See where the win's blowin'. The head don't deserve booin'.

CRAGGE: *(Dead cold.)* I said that, did I?

ADAMS: *(Very much to the point.)* Well, if 'e deserves booin' boo then.

BROOK: 'E'd rather lick up to them. 'E needs a job.

CRAGGE: Yeah, I got more use for 'im than you lot. There's nothin' between mates. *(In cold blood to COLMAN.)* The best time between us as mates was at Trafalgar Square, New Year's Eve. We 'ad the fountain spray in our faces and talked a lot. That's all I can remember about it. That the talk was fabulous and the mood was sweet, and that if I could a had a girl instead a you I would a swapped. In fact we'd gone out lookin' for girls. So even when you was me mate I'd a swapped you for your sister or playing a big match.

COLMAN: Yeah, that's all you would bloody remember.

CRAGGE: *(In the same vein.)* And if you leave 'ere and got on, then we'd talk if we met, unless I see you first then I'd dodge 'cos I couldn't be bothered; or 'cos I hated you for what you got.

ADAMS: 'E wouldn't mind that. If 'e got it.

CRAGGE: *That's* the God's truth as well. And if I'd become a footballer you lot would be just crowds to clap me and bawl out me name, then let out to work for the next fare. That's the gang of us.

BROOK: *(To CRAGGE.)* Go and tell 'eadmaster we booed 'im.

CRAGGE: I won't 'ave to. You ain't gonna stop broadcastin' it till it gets back to him.

BROOK: Say you never done it. Rat.

COLMAN: 'E done it. It's the gang of us.

CRAGGE: *(Deep pessimism.)* Yeah, and 'e'll kick me out, deny it or not, I know it.

COLMAN: *(Jeering.)* There's always night-school.

There is an announcement over the tannoy: 'The following boys will report to the head's study immediately: Brook, Adams, Colman, Cragge, Jordan.'

JORDAN: *(Rushing in.)* Helen's in a patrol-van at the back of the school.

BROOK: She ain't you know.

JORDAN: We ain't 'ere.

BROOK: Let's go out by the fence.

JORDAN: Ain't you comin'?

CRAGGE: I'm clean.

ADAMS: 'E wants to nark.

CRAGGE: When I nark you kill me.

BROOK: Helen will tell the law you were there. I'll make 'er tell 'em you had 'er, so they'll take anything you say with salt.

CRAGGE: Try anything you like. I stop 'ere.

BROOK: Didn't you say 'e'll kick you out. You don't believe what your brains tell you, d'ya! *(He moves in.)*

CRAGGE: You know I been had up once for defendin' meself, so you won't hit me again, will you.

JORDAN: He knows we booed him.

CRAGGE: I didn't boo.

BROOK: 'E wants to rat.

JORDAN: You kept your 'and 'idden.

COLMAN: Didn't you just.

BROOK: You suck.

They exit leaving CRAGGE. A moment after the HEADMASTER enters.

HEAD: *(To CRAGGE.)* Where are the others?

CRAGGE: I dunno. Gone.

HEAD: Gone, eh? Well I've caught you.

CRAGGE: I didn't boo.

HEAD: I know you. Into Assembly.

CRAGGE: I didn't boo. You'll never believe me.

HEAD: I'll never know if you booed; but you're the sort I must make an example of to this school before I hand you over elsewhere. You swear, you smoke, your mind's filthy. You or your friends booed me last night in front of the Governors... I'll burn it into your backside for the school to see that I'll not be disgraced.

CRAGGE: *(Almost unable to speak.)* I want to stay here at least to get on wiv the newspaper.

HEAD: And to go on corrupting the school with filth. The public don't read our magazines; they see your conduct. The Governors won't blame me if you never get G.C.E. God is responsible for your brains but I give you your character... *(Hardly able to speak with anger.)* The Assembly is waiting.

CRAGGE: I didn't boo.

HEAD: Into Assembly.

CRAGGE: *(Raging.)* I didn't boo.

HEAD: Get in.

CRAGGE: *(Wearily.)* If I stay it's gonna be the same. It ain't gonna be different. What 'ave I got out of it 'ere. What if I 'adn't come then. I could still do what you expect me to be doin', hauling Whitbread's when I ain't actually doin' porridge… My dad's a fool, me own mum says that, and I ain't gonna go his road. I got brains and my mum don't want me there. What about your kid? *(Scornfully.)* What's his brains? Why is it that the likes a me are the ones fillin' jails. Why me, why not 'im?

HEAD: He's in the school here like you.

CRAGGE: He won't be in bloody Whitbread.

HEAD: You swear at me, boy?

CRAGGE: Me dad says it and it just slipped out. I wanna stay so I take it back.

HEAD: *(Flicking his hand.)* In. For the last time.

CRAGGE: For sayin' bloody I'll 'ave it in 'ere.

HEAD: You'll obey while you're here. You won't stand there dictating.

CRAGGE: Lots to boo about, ain't there?

HEAD: Frankly boy, the sort you are, if you touched a daughter of mine I'd strangle you. Go to the police. Get out.

CRAGGE: You're willin' to send blokes out, ain't you? You'd 'ave blokes put out. Yeah, though jobs that are prison to 'em, or the prisons are waitin'. Alright. I'll have it from you. I'll 'ave it from you, then I'll talk to them. I'm clean, and if you're clean you're O.K. with 'em. Most times. I'm straight. No fear. I'm gonna be in them papers.

The HEAD puts on his cap and gown, and addresses the audience.

HEAD: Be quiet, boys. Last night, as you must all have heard by now, something unprecedented happened in this school. Boys booed while I, their headmaster, was talking. This in the presence of guests.

A murmur in the hall.

Silence, please. *(Immediately more severe.)* I am not going to say who the boys are but I'm going to say what they are. They are, briefly, scum. Such boys we have no use for, and I am glad to say they are all but perhaps one of them leaving the school. *(Milder again.)* They have no use for us. They will be happier outside. I sincerely hope they will remain 'outside' and are never sent 'inside'.

Some who have caught the joke laugh.

School was for them a sort of prison.

The rest laugh, having caught on.

Hooliganism, rowdyism, these will never be tolerated. Come here, Cragge. Bend over.

As CRAGGE bends over and HEADMASTER raises his cane, the lights begin to fade. And the strokes are heard in the dark.

The End.

WHITE WITCH

White Witch

The play is loosely connected with a Jamaican legend of Annie Palmer, mistress of the Rose Hall plantation, who is said to have murdered four husbands and had many lovers. Reckord sets what he has called 'a bloodstained comedy' on a Jamaican plantation early in the nineteenth century.

White and wealthy Simon Palmer, who has fathered children with slaves, marries Annie, the daughter of a duke, and brings her from England to produce for him a legal white heir. The marriage agreement is a business transaction between Palmer and the duke. The buyer works relentlessly to impregnate his purchase, but she has multiple miscarriages on the voyage to the Caribbean. By the time she lands in Jamaica there is a rumour that Annie may be a witch. As Chloe, one of Palmer's discarded lovers, declares, 'Babies are a blessing from heaven, a gift from above, a benediction by Almighty God, and witches never carry these little angels for long.'

How much is merely rumour? What are the facts? Has Annie, like some of the slave women, been taking powders to induce abortions? Is she really a witch? She herself informs us early that, back in England, when two of her brothers burned to death in a barn after killing a stable-lad who was her lover, 'there was talk of murder by witchcraft' and she was married off to Mr Palmer. 'My dear it was the dock or the altar. I had to leave the country to evade arrest.' Palmer doesn't know all this at first, and is more and more disturbed by the stories he hears.

Annie is a disruptive element on the plantation, where women exist for the pleasure of men and to bear them children. Women, even white women, are an underclass, somewhat analogous to slaves; but 'milady's brought rebellion with her. Disorder and confusion.' Mistress of the great house, she makes common cause with slaves, confiding with some of the women like their equal and openly seducing black men. She submits to Palmer's sexual labours but is determined not to have children for him, and she often addresses him in a manner implying superiority.

ANNIE: Today my lord came home from the wars, and pleasured me twice in his topboots.

PALMER: Which wars?

ANNIE: It's a quotation sir.

PALMER: Kneel down, but I mustn't be long.

ANNIE: *(Kneels, resting on the bed.)* You're seldom up for long sir.

PALMER: I never know when you mock me.

Her sexual aggression is seen as unacceptable. Though black or mulatto women may be lively in bed, a white woman must not seem to enjoy sex. 'Pleasure,' says old Dr Baillie, 'is not part of the divine prescription. See to it she lies perfectly still, and with her eyes shut.' But as Annie tells a black man she has targeted, 'Witches have fought for centuries for carnal insurrection.' She is in tune with the blacks (deemed animals by Dr Baillie and by Palmer). As she and Lucinda (a young slave woman) say to and with each other, the black God summoned from Africa by fierce drumming on the plantation is 'Bigger than bakkra...and we take him and grind him and possess him...And grab his back and shudder...And God sinting stand up well strong...And never go down...Till he pleasure us...And free us.'

Belief may free their minds, but their bodies are plantation property. 'You think I went clear to England for a mule?' Palmer, enraged, asks Annie. 'No,' she replies, 'clearly you went for a breeding slave.' Crassly as ever, he insists: 'I'm going to man you and breed you and lock you up for nine months till you drop, and nine months after that, one a year, till my quiver's full. So help me God.' When a slave gets ground up with cane at the mill ('Joko's blood make good rum') discussion centres on how much he was worth, and on the failure to save something of the investment by severing his arm in good time.

The dead, however, walk free – 'who can chain up the dead?' Much that challenges the *status quo* is attributed to the ghost of Herrera, an executed rebel. Annie, with supernatural insight, sees him returning whole. 'What a torso. And there's his bleeding head. I have no idea how I'll get those two together... Yes, I think I know.' Annie says that when she was only twelve she 'started seeing the dead walk.' She envisions Palmer's end. There are other suggestions that she is, as rumoured, a witch. Immediately after she hears her husband's horse gallop away, she bears a candle-lit breast to the young Jamaican black man she intends to seduce. Even if we take drowning and flying to be sexual metaphors, we are also invited to place her as a witch.

ANNIE: You daren't tell, and I daren't tell.

RHONE: Right here quick.

ANNIE: Come to the sea, and swim in it.

RHONE: We can do everything right here quick.

ANNIE: I want to play. *(She strokes it with her toe.)*

RHONE: *(Drowning.)* I have my life. I have a woman.

ANNIE: She has black breasts, with purple nipples.

RHONE: *(Grabbing at her.)* Sea too far.

ANNIE: I'm a witch. Fly me.

What being a witch may mean is one of the questions raised in the play. According to Dr Baillie, 'Witches have conspired in bed against us from the days of Eve and the snake… Sex and witchcraft is one word.' Annie knows these views. She tells us: 'when I was ten things flew around my room. Doctors said my carnal feelings were inflamed.' She sees hostility to 'witches' as bound up with the historical subjugation of women. 'For every malady of woman there's a leaf in the forest, and the wise women who searched for them for centuries to stop their own pain and enjoy their desires, were called witches and burnt, and their knowledge destroyed.'

The play argues lustily against repression. The repressive extreme is represented by Dr Baillie, his fraudulence exposed in 'speaking medically'. Told that Annie 'thrashes about' during coitus, he wants to know if she has pleasure in it. 'Yes, doc. You mustn't ask me again,' says Palmer. 'But, speaking medically, does she actually enjoy it?' 'Yes doc.' 'Even revel in it?' 'Yes, doc.' 'You should have a word with the bishop. This may be wickedness.' At the liberated extreme promoted by the play, Annie, who fears 'that the sexually disturbed rule the world,' quotes Blake's *The Garden of Love*, disapproving of 'priests in black gowns…binding with briars [our] joys and desires.' As a child she left home and lived with religious free-thinkers and free-lovers, who raised their children in common and gave them the time and affection they needed. The result, she says, was 'the children weren't mean in their affection, and were naturally carnal with each other.' In a ritual sequence, to the sound of talking drums, when Abuku, Lucinda and Annie shed their clothes, Annie invokes 'Satan, fallen angel of joy, fallen angel of love' and they '*kiss each others' mons*', chanting 'I see the body of Christ, neither sinful nor crucified.' Annie would turn great houses into schools, and 'bring children back to their senses.' Pun intended. 'There ought,' says Annie, 'to be a Royal Society for the protection of sensual children.'

White Witch proffers nudity, seductions, sexual humiliation, murder (a dagger in the groin), ghosts, madness and other challenges, and a lot of activity establishing the troubled plantation context. There is mention of ambushes and fear that rebellion may spread from Santo Domingo. Orders are given for punishment by whipping, cutting, hanging. Distrust is palpable. 'You must wear shoes milady, so people can hear you.' House-slaves get called 'safe-niggers', but 'Are the safe-niggers safe?' People talk in glances and whispers. African drumming is an insistent background, frenzied from time to time. A good production will make the audience see and feel the accelerating chaos in the great house, and the disintegration of Palmer.

While Palmer unravels, Annie projects unchanging self-assurance. Her role requires charismatic sexual presence and a playful intelligence. Cupid, with 'a nose for dark truth,' is the only character who can keep up with her in intellectual discourse. He 'spends his life in his head,' living 'in the deep hell of yes and no and yes again.' His mother, Princess considers him irresolute: 'Do something for the liberty you prate about!' she exhorts. Annie, in contrast, is glad 'he isn't a blind creature of his time, passing down tried and tested lies.'

Other roles are variously rewarding, with complexities to make real. Princess, dignified mother of Cupid, Palmer's 'favourite bastard', dispenses a powder to induce abortions and is organizing a slave revolt. Her husband, Sammy, extravagantly subservient to Palmer (perhaps playing fool to catch wise), stays loyal to Princess until the pressure proves too much. Beautiful Chloe, a shade-conscious young mulatto who has slept with Palmer and Cupid, spies on Annie while pretending to serve her faithfully. Rhone, commanded into sexual service, is vividly fearful and then pathetically jealous. Dr Baillie ('I'll look at her clitoris... Amputation may be necessary') is a richly repulsive cameo role. The Machiavellian Dawes manipulates nearly everybody, including Palmer, and announces his need for 'sensual refinements' and a predilection towards rape – 'If I can get it, I don't want it...Your tail must say yes, and your mouth must demurely say no.' Chloe has heard 'unmentionable things' about him.

When *The White Witch of Rose Hall* was staged in Kingston, Jamaica, late in 1975 reviewers, though reporting some disgusted responses, were not troubled by sex and violence and the supernatural. They recognized the play as entertaining, suspenseful and vibrant with ideas. The version printed here was given a reading in London at the Tricycle Theatre early in 1980s. It will be good to see a full production of this newer, tighter script.

Mervyn Morris

The White Witch of Rose Hall was first performed Sunday October 4th 1975 at the Creative Arts Centre, University of the West Indies, Mona Campus, Jamaica directed by Lloyd Reckord with the following cast:

CHLOE, Cyrene Tomlinson
PALMER, Thom Cross
DAWES, Volier Johnson
ANNIE PALMER, Sally Carey
RHONE, Samuel Walker
DOCTOR, Michael Reckord
BEA, Lorraine Smith/Beverly Marsh
CUPID, Trenton Allen
PRINCESS, Pauline Stone
SAMMY, Clive Walker
ATTORNEY, Barry Reckord
LEADER OF RUNAWAYS, Ronald Goshop

Set Designer, Colin Garland/Pat Stanigar
Costume Designer, Colin Garland
Lighting Designer, George Carter
Sound, Evan Williams

Text: *White Witch* is from the London production in 1985.

Characters

ANNIE PALMER
A young English lady

SIMON PALMER
White Jamaican in his thirties

CUPID
Young Mulatto

DAWES
Middle-aged Mulatto

PRINCESS
Black Jamaican in her thirties

RHONE
Black Jamaican. Late twenties

CHLOE
Beautiful young Mulatto

SAMMY
Middle-aged Black

DR. BAILLIE
Elderly Scot

LUCINDA
Young Black Jamaican

ABUKU
Young Black Jamaican

HERRERA
Young Black Jamaican

Place: Jamaica

Time: 1800

Note: There are three playing areas: the drawing-room of Rose Hall, *PALMER*'s great-house, sparsely but beautifully furnished, with a highly polished mahogany floor; stairs leading up to *ANNIE*'s bedroom, and the bedroom itself; and a courtyard.

Act One

Rose Hall great-house. Drawing room. Two slaves whispering.

ABUKU: I hear she was a terror. Even before she had breasts on 'er.

LUCINDA: I hear worse.

ABUKU: *(Hearing CHLOE about to enter.)* If we don't ask all will be revealed.

CHLOE enters.

CHLOE: The rumours Abuku! Lucinda, the rumours!

LUCINDA: Miss Chloe, if I listen to rumours bakkra will sell me.

ABUKU: And send me back to the slave-gang.

CHLOE: Criminal conversations no less.

LUCINDA: What is that?

CHLOE: I don't know what that is, and it is not to pass my lips, but she miscarried on the boat, and she will miscarry again. Babies are a blessing from heaven, a gift from above, a benediction by Almighty God, and witches can never carry those little angels for long. She come straight from hell.

ABUKU: I hear she come straight from England, and I want to go there right now, right now.

CHLOE: *(Sharply, to ABUKU.)* Fan the room. Lucinda, what you doin' down here?

Before ABUKU can use his giant fan, PALMER comes roaring down the stairs and both slaves vanish. PALMER complains about the African song drifting in from the garden.

PALMER: Chloe.

CHLOE: Yes bakkra.

PALMER: Mrs. Palmer's asleep. Tell the gardeners to stop the blasted nyeng-nyeng. And Chloe...

CHLOE: Yes bakkra.

PALMER: I know the whole estate want to gawp at the wife but she's just arrive and she must rest. She's breeding and I want Dr. Baillie to see her through the first months. But she say she don't believe in doctors.

CHLOE: *(Darkly.)* What she believe in?

PALMER: She grew wild like love-bush. Not brought up. Not much broughtupcy. Her house in England is full of niggers, and she sketched every black sailor on the boat. Her father is a madman. A wit and a poet. Left her at school in Paris during the revolution.

CHLOE: Well bakkra I knew the first second she landed off the boat.

PALMER: How?

CHLOE: Ghosts ran like rats through the house.

PALMER: *(Rubbing her arse, mocking her.)* Chloe I better put your tongue in me mouth.

CHLOE: All of a sudden the house is haunted. Bakkra, milady's brought rebellion with her. Disorder and confusion. A witch can make her very thoughts come to pass. Nobody's safe. She will change your luck. From this very day your luck change for she's delinquent and will corrupt everybody round her. Witches are fearless.

PALMER: You're jealous I brought back a wife?

CHLOE: Bakkra meetin' a witch is a dreadful accident, like runnin' into a coach and four. She will kill you.

PALMER: I lie down with her. You're jealous of that?

CHLOE: You lay with me but you never pleasured me.

PALMER: No? My wife took to me like a shark to a slave-ship. Turned up her pretty white belly before the wedding.

CHLOE: Poor Mrs. Palmer. I hope you pleasure her. But bakkra if you pleasure a witch your testicles swell up big big and huge like The Roman Empire, and you have to carry 'em behind you in a barrel.

ABUKU enters with PALMER'S riding-whip and hat, and helps him finish dressing.

PALMER: *(Fondling CHLOE.)* So who rudeness you while I was away?

CHLOE: Nobody sir. You talk naked like this to Mrs. Palmer sir?

PALMER: Lawd, Chloe no. I set me mouth and talk British. Me jaw tired. And me money ran away like hog-fat. That marriage settlement, lawd, if I die everything is hers and any child she has.

DAWES enters.

DAWES: That is an incitement to murder.

PALMER: If I die she's the richest woman in England. But Dawes, lawd, I couldn't get her for less, and I didn't go so far to bring back a crow. I'm certain of one thing, that I, Simon Palmer, bring back the most aristocratic lady ever to park her arse in a great-house.

DAWES: And bakkra she prettier than money.

PALMER: But Chloe, tek warning, her spirit's high. She passed the time gunning down rats on the boat.

DAWES: Well bakkra I can't imagine her going to a school for ladies and not learning how to poison a chalice or handle a pistol. I hear on the boat she wanted to bathe over the side like the sailors. Naked.

CHLOE: When they're arustocratic they not too ladylike.

DAWES: You must say aristocratic.

PALMER: Chloe arusto or aristo she must rest. She miscarried once already on the boat. Too much excitement.

DAWES: She's breeding again?

PALMER: Yes. Night and day I was down there. Nothing else to do on the boat. My son will be the richest commoner in England. So mek her sit down on the couch and rest. She can sketch. Dawes I want you to introduce Mrs. Palmer to protocol. Tell her no dancing with coachmen. Tell her if you dance with niggers, they peep into your grave. And make arrangements for her ball. Invite members of the Assembly from all over the island. Let them come see the quality I bring back. Her mother dropped twelve.

DAWES: She is good breedin' stock.

PALMER: Her sister died in child-bed, but her dam and sire are good. One granny dropped thirteen.

DAWES: Her pedigree's good.

CHLOE: Bakkra your field-slaves are not breedin'.

DAWES: They goin' to the witches for powders. I just arrest one. Come and sentence her.

PALMER: Dawes, I want you to wipe out every witch from this property.

DAWES: Stone them bakkra?

PALMER: Stone them, hang them, strangle them, anything, but terrify the bitches.

DAWES: Come and pass sentence. And we're startin' work on the new shit-pit. Come and look at it.

PALMER and DAWES exit in one direction, and CHLOE in another. Lights on ANNIE, in her bedroom, talking to LUCINDA.

LUCINDA: If you're morning sick milady drink this.

ANNIE drinks.

Twelve weeks on a rolling boat. What a journey.

ANNIE: *(Looking out to sea.)* But colour is mined in the seas here. The waves run with it, the clouds draw it up. It tints the very moon… Do those men with dogs guard the house day and night?

LUCINDA: They're safe-niggers. Promoted from the field.

ANNIE: They must be very wicked to get promoted. Were you promoted?

LUCINDA: Yes. I was wicked milady.

ANNIE: Then you must have gone, like me, to a convent.

LUCINDA: I was in the kitchen, and bakkra told me to kneel down.

ANNIE: *(Laughing.)* And will you still?

LUCINDA: I know not the position now. You and Miss Chloe might bear the brunt.

ANNIE: My dear men say we go to bed for love or money. Never for the real thing.

LUCINDA: I go to bed to sleep milady.

ANNIE laughs.

ANNIE: And breed dear. If sex be conquest and men the conquerors, what's in it for women but submission and babies.

LUCINDA: I have three.

ANNIE: Where are they?

LUCINDA: Miss Chloe can't breed, she's a mule, and she was jealous of my three so bakkra sell them.

Appalled silence.

They're in San Domingo, and there's rebellion. Please don't mention them again. We spoke in confidence.

ANNIE: *Do* we speak in confidence?

LUCINDA: If you tell bakkra, he will send me back to the slave gang.

ANNIE: I once exchanged confidences with a stable lad.

LUCINDA: He betrayed them?

ANNIE: He left marks on my body to prove to his friends that he'd shagged me.

LUCINDA: Were you in love with him?

ANNIE: Yes. So my brothers spat on me, and pitch-forked the stable-lad.

LUCINDA: Did he die?

ANNIE: Yes. So God punished them.

LUCINDA: Did they die?

ANNIE: Two slavers less.

LUCINDA: How did they die?

ANNIE: Burned to death in a barn. Sometimes, occasionally, very occasionally, brutes die painfully. One of the few thoughts I find bearable.

LUCINDA: Were you near the barn?

ANNIE. No. But when I was ten things flew around my room. Doctors said my carnal feelings were inflamed, and there were one or two happenings later on. So I left home and lived with the ravers, religious free-thinkers and free-lovers. I am not religious, but I liked the way they raised their children in common, and so could give them all the time and affection they needed. The result was the children weren't mean in their affection, and were naturally carnal with each other. But this was obviously a 'den of iniquity', though the children had carnal knowledge among themselves, not with elders. So when the barn burnt to a cinder, with my brothers in it, there was talk of murder by witchcraft, and I was married off to Mr. Palmer.

LUCINDA: How could you marry a slaver?

ANNIE: Struth, you know the drill. All the money for sons, not a guinea for daughters. So I could have been a poor and persecuted raver, a slavey for my aunt the bald duchess, or marry a cocksy rich man. Why, I didn't even smell his stockings. Then they dressed me up fit to kill, came with praise from far and near, so here I am, meant to spawn a dozen slavers.

LUCINDA: I wish I knew you Miss Annie.

ANNIE: *(Coming clean.)* My dear it was the dock or the altar. I had to leave the country to evade arrest.

LUCINDA: That's the rumour.

ANNIE: *(Fiercely.)* My lover was murdered and nobody charged.

LUCINDA: Did you ever love your brothers?

ANNIE: They were kind in little ways, and hideous in large. Believed wars are just and slavery necessary. I've always found human-beings confusing, if I assume they are human. Now I assume two out of three people are sheep, and will bury me in sheep-shit that deep. That's my guiding truth, and it isn't arrogance but despair; though I don't mean to be buried.

LUCINDA: It's a wonder Mr. Palmer didn't hear the rumours.

ANNIE: He was too dazzled by my connections. We met and married in a month.

LUCINDA: What will happen when he hears them?

ANNIE: *(Dry.)* He knows witches can't breed... What happened to your babies' father?

LUCINDA: He ran away.

ANNIE: Are you still in love with him?

LUCINDA: *(Averting her eyes.)* He's a rebel.

ANNIE: What was his name?

LUCINDA: Herrera. Why was? Is he dead? You read the future?

ANNIE: And wonder who writes it.

LUCINDA: Herrera went mad with hunger in the drought and joined the rebels. When you love them it's awful. The love thing is awful. *(Distressed.)* You trust your vision? Is Herrera dead?

ANNIE: Never trust visions my lovely darling. Crude reality wins in the end. *(Migrating birds pass over.)* Look. Magic guides migrating birds. Such powers have faded in men. My nice brother experiments with electricity, and will light up the world, but we live in psychic darkness. All hit and miss. Not scientific. The day I married I saw a hole being dug near this house. I knew it was my husband's grave. I was wrong.

LUCINDA: They're digging a new shit-pit. They're just startin' it.

ANNIE: Dear God it will be my own grave. I feel ill. My sister died in child-bed and I'm six weeks on. I need a powder.

LUCINDA: That is death milady.

ANNIE: I must get one.

LUCINDA: How did you abort on the boat?

ANNIE: I got powders from the ravers. They don't last.

LUCINDA: Speak to Princess.

ANNIE: Princess?

LUCINDA: She's the housekeeper. Speak to her.

ANNIE: Tell me about her.

LUCINDA: Her husband is keeper of the stores, and she made him buy extra food for the slaves during the drought, and when bakkra finds out he'll be in danger. Princess wants slavery abolished. If you need a powder speak to her.

PALMER re-enters drawing-room with DAWES. He shouts "Miss Annie, Miss Annie".

DAWES: Tall rum bakkra?

PALMER: Tall rum.

CHLOE: You want food?

PALMER: My belly's unsettled. Coming over Mt. Diablo, road wet and slippery, the horse nearly pitched me over the precipice.

ANNIE sweeps down the stairs.

ANNIE: *(Dry wit.)* A widow? At twenty?

PALMER: Horse pitched and nearly killed me and she laughed.

ANNIE: *(Hugging him.)* No more bragging and prating about the great horseman he is.

PALMER: Couldn't you sleep?

ANNIE: Isn't it time the black men stopped drumming?

PALMER: You hear them. You hear the welcome back we get from the niggers.

ANNIE: I hear the women refuse to breed.

CHLOE: They want to grind ma'am but they don't want to breed.

ANNIE: *(Dry.)* Oh that's wicked of them. Proper slaves would breed without grinding.

PALMER: *(Laughing.)* She comes from a great reformin' family like me. *(Of DAWES and CHLOE.)* I promote black people. I wouldn't marry 'em but I promote and use 'em.

DAWES: *(Of the drumming.)* This drumming is not forbidden milady. We allow this.

PALMER: It's the mosquitoes that will serenade us to death.

ANNIE: I hear them singing.

CHLOE: It's not sing they singing, it's cry they crying, for blood mam.

PALMER: Chloe will look after you.

CHLOE: My father was an old soldier man, from England, so I'm not too dark. I cleaned out your room from top to toe, me same one, so neither spider nor scorpion will creep and crawl.

PALMER: And this is Dawes. Dawes is my right hand.

DAWES: You must wear shoes milady, so people can hear you.

ANNIE looks at him gravely.

PALMER: Her grandfather was a slave-trader. And the family crest has two niggers on it. Come give me a kiss Miss Annie and I'm gone.

ANNIE: May I come with you to see the estates?

PALMER: No. Lawd, you're so pretty, you must bring me luck.

ANNIE: Pretty is lucky, is it?

PRINCESS enters with pork.

PALMER: Princess, jerk-pork in England was no pork to pork in this house. *(To ANNIE.)* Princess is my house-keeper.

PRINCESS bows.

They don't know jerk-pork. All they know is abolition.

PRINCESS: *(As PALMER belches.)* And good English manners.

PALMER: And you know how loud I can get. I can get very loud. They thought only a fool could be as loud as me.

PRINCESS: *(Dry.)* Till they saw your carriage.

PALMER: Her son is my favourite bastard. *(Shouts.)* Cupid. Where the hell is the boy?

CUPID enters.

You are sixteen years old. You should be planting good seed, not sulkin' all over the estate. You should learn how to handle women. Your mother gave way to Chloe and several betwixt and between, yet there is no contention among any of 'em. You can write that on my grave. He ground women and cane and ground 'em well. Chloe, tell Mrs. Palmer how many bastards I have. Octoroon, quadroon, every kind of coon. But this *(CUPID.)* is my favourite one. *(To PRINCESS.)* Where is your man Sammy?

PRINCESS: Waiting to greet you sir.

PALMER: Abuku call Mass Sammy. And call Rhone.

PALMER is silent, waiting for SAMMY, creating great tension. ANNIE gazes at PRINCESS.

PALMER: Dawes, give me that bill. *(DAWES hands it to him.)*

SAMMY: *(To ANNIE, bowing.)* I am Sammy milady. Keeper of the stores, Princess's husband, Cupid's step-father, and your humble servant, blessing the marriage.

ANNIE: *(Smiling.)* Marriage needs every blessing.

SAMMY: Mornin' bakkra. And respect sir.

RHONE: *(To PALMER.)* My respect sir.

PALMER: Sammy look at this bill.

SAMMY: Yes bakkra.

PALMER: Tell me what it is about.

SAMMY: Food sir.

PALMER: Dawes tell me you ordered salt beef and salt pork for the niggers in my absence.

SAMMY: Drought burn up the ground since you gone, and nutten grow. Even the few goats drop down from hunger and thirst.

PALMER: So you order salt beef and salt pork for the niggers.

SAMMY: They were starving bakkra so I got feeding for them. Worst drought in memory.

PALMER: You told Dawes?

SAMMY: No bakkra. That is not Dawes' department. I bought it the day you married, to bless the marriage with feeding.

PALMER: A bill for fifty pounds to bless the marriage. Chloe will tell me it's an omen!

SAMMY: Well bakkra, rebellion is spreading from Santo Domingo. I had to decide. You don't see the welcome you get from the people.

PALMER: You know they must feed themselves from the ample grounds I give them.

SAMMY: *(Repeating.)* From the ample grounds you give them.

PALMER: And you know that since sugar duty rise and price fall, one hundred estates in Jamaica shut down. And slaves are wandering around. A danger to us.

SAMMY: Bakkra I know.

PALMER: Yet you order salt beef and salt pork from the Jews? They greased your palm?

SAMMY: Me? Sammy? Bakkra, 400 hogshead the niggers produce. The grub well earned.

PALMER: Their Sunday market shut down?

SAMMY: They're selling food still, yes bakkra, but little or nutten.

PALMER: They sell their own food and eat mine.

SAMMY: Bakkra they were hungry, and raised rass, and called for feeding.

PALMER: Dawes.

DAWES: Yes bakkra.

PALMER: Put Sammy up for sale.

CUPID: But they were hungry.

SAMMY: *(Prostrating.)* Mercy bakkra.

CUPID: The fire in Santo Domingo will burn down Jamaica.

PALMER: Liberty, equality, fraternity is a belching fart. That won't bankrupt me.

DAWES: *(Kicking SAMMY.)* Come old man. *(Strips him of keys.)*

PALMER: *(Throwing RHONE keys.)* Rhone, take over the stores. And take Sammy out.

RHONE exits with SAMMY.

PALMER: I've come back to taxation, bankruptcies, rebellion. I've had so many anxious hours this year I would not wish the same again for double the profit I may get, if any. But now I have a wife, and a son coming up.

DAWES: *(Passing round drinks for a toast.)* God bless 'em.

CHLOE: *(With a little curtsey and hand-clap.)* God protect 'em.

PALMER: Health and long life Miss Annie. (*To CUPID, who isn't cheering.)* Raise your glass.

DAWES: Bakkra, what will make him a winner?

PALMER: Energy, man, like my father. He had more energy for detail than other men. There was no joy in the man but he could add one and one. I want my son to be born feet first, like that old man. *(A toast.)* My son will dine with dukes.

DAWES: And they will envy his money and write down his discourse.

PALMER: Yes Dawes, my son will be the richest commoner in England... Chloe they cook a royal dinner for milady?

CHLOE: Tea, coffee, claret, hock-negus, madeira, sangaree, hot and cold meats, stews and fries, hot and cold fish, pickled and plain, peppers, gingers, sweet-meats, acid-fruit and sweet-jellies.

ANNIE: It's too hot for a greasy feast. *(Ready to vomit.)*

PALMER: *(Embraces ANNIE.)* Oh my wife fattens my eyes. We took long walks and lay a-bed. Gave large gifts and little presents. She's turned my life round. Before I met her I'd wake up feeling like a double-blank. Not a state you want to describe.

ANNIE: *(Dry.)* I arrived on a bad day. *(RHONE re-enters.)*

PALMER: Rhone, I'm going to my estate at Ramble. Any trouble, call out the militia. Miss Annie, I'm gone. If you want a boy to fan you, tell Rhone.

RHONE bows and exits, followed by everybody except PALMER and ANNIE. As CUPID and PRINCESS exit, they share a private toast.

PRINCESS: *(Of ANNIE.)* May she die in child-bed. *(Exit.)*

CUPID: May she die in childbed.

PALMER: *(To ANNIE.)* You talk to Cupid. The blasted missionaries teach 'em rebellion. We must restrain 'em. If they didn't rebel, we wouldn't have to murder them.

ANNIE: Let Sammy stay in his house till he's sold.

PALMER: That's for me to say milady.

ANNIE: You'll correct me if I'm wrong. But if we have so much more of everything than the slaves, they might start murdering us for a change.

PALMER: If I lost every shilling down a nigger's maw, it would cat and kitten its way back to me, and tomorrow we'd be rich again. I don't say the niggers are lazy, but they're born ignorant, and when they're not they rise like Dawes.

ANNIE: Free Sammy from the dungeons till he's sold.

PALMER: *(Gazing at her.)* Love mixed with business troubles men's fortunes.

ANNIE: *(Gazing at him.)* Are you in danger?

PALMER: I'll tell Dawes to leave Sammy in his house.

Both exit. HERRERA the rebel, armed with a machete, steals into the house.

LUCINDA: *(Standing at the top of the stairs, sees him; whispers.)* Herrera

She runs down the stairs and hugs him. PRINCESS enters with a suckling pig in a basket.

PRINCESS: *(To HERRERA, hissing.)* Make haste.

LUCINDA runs back upstairs. HERRERA puts the suckling in a crocus-bag, and flees as CUPID enters.

PRINCESS: Great God, I feared it was Dawes.

CUPID: How did he get past the safe-niggers?

PRINCESS: Are the safe-niggers safe?

CUPID: *(Angry.)* You feed runaways?

PRINCESS: Sammy is for sale and you do nothing?

CUPID: *(Rage.)* I didn't know my mother was a criminal. *(He starts to exit, then turns and desperately hugs her.)* Thank God you haven't been caught. You must stop.

PRINCESS: Do something for the liberty you prate about!

She exits and CUPID follows, trying to reason with her.

ANNIE: *(Off, to PALMER.)* Safe ride.

PALMER: *(Off.)* I'm tempted to tarry. I'm right up on tiptoe.

They re-enter the drawing-room, and go upstairs to the bedroom.

ANNIE: Today my lord came home from the wars, and pleasured me twice in his topboots.

PALMER: Which wars?

ANNIE: It's a quotation sir.

PALMER: Kneel down, but I mustn't be long.

ANNIE: *(Kneels, resting on the bed.)* You're seldom up for long sir.

PALMER: I never know when you mock me. *(He shoots off and blames her.)* I feel mocked and spill it. Why do you mock me?

DAWES: (*Off, shouts to PALMER.)* Bakkra, bakkra, come quick.

ANNIE: *(Laughing.)* Tell him you have.

PALMER: *(Angrily.)* No more mockery!

DAWES: *(Off.)* Bakkra they catch the rebel Herrera.

PALMER runs out. In the courtyard, RHONE, surrounded by a crowd off-stage, disgorges HERRERA from a crocus-bag.

VOICE: *(Off.)* Is me Joko, ketch him. Me Joko. Bakkra prize-nigger. Herrera is you one born, and is you one goin dead.

VOICES: Cut 'im. Cut 'im.

HERRERA: *(Whinnying with fright.)* Don't make dem cut me.

DAWES puts a gun to HERRERA'S head.

PALMER: Fire!

DAWES fires, and HERRERA drops.

DAWES: *(To RHONE.)* Feed the dogs.

RHONE carries off the body. Dogs, off, start whining.

Lights on ANNIE, in her bedroom, holding LUCINDA who is sobbing. And on PRINCESS and CUPID downstairs standing shell-shocked.

ANNIE: Show these merchants the terror they bring, and they burn witches, love their wives, and count dividend.

PRINCESS: *(Looking out the window, to CUPID.)* If they kill him today, they can't kill him tomorrow. Join the rebellion.

CUPID, troubled, exits as ANNIE comes downstairs.

ANNIE: *(To PRINCESS.)* My husband has agreed to leave Sammy in his house.

PRINCESS: *(Bowing.)* I owe you favours.

ANNIE: Princess, this is no ménage for an innocent and I'm six weeks on. I need a powder to get rid of the richest commoner in England.

PRINCESS: Here we get rid of husband and child, or we only get planted again.

ANNIE: Funny, I saw him dead by now. It's the only reason I married him. I saw his death, then lost it.

PRINCESS: It's one thing marrying a man, hoping he'll die, but actually to have seen him stone dead...

ANNIE: I feel cold-blooded about slavers.

PRINCESS: You want five estates.

ANNIE: If I must choose between being slaver or slave.
Hungry or overfed. Does he always ride with armed men?

PRINCESS: He walks alone at night on the estate.

ANNIE: I seldom missed the rats on the boat.

PRINCESS: Guns are noisy and flash in the pan. Milady would hang.

ANNIE: It wasn't the way I saw him die.

PRINCESS: Who killed him?

ANNIE: Was he killed or driven mad? Did his mind go?

PRINCESS: His heart? Broken?

ANNIE: It was one end of him or another.

PRINCESS: *(Droll.)* Not his eggs.

ANNIE: Surely that would have been unforgettable. Do get me a powder my dear, and send Rhone in.

PRINCESS: Rhone is a man who hasn't suffered and causes suffering.

ANNIE: Please send him in.

PRINCESS bows and exits. ANNIE lights up a lovely clay pipe. CHLOE enters with coffee.

CHLOE: You saw what happen mam? I was busy drawing coffee and miss everything. *(ANNIE is silent.)* You can get a cool bath, sweet and scented, with lime and orange blossom. You want a drink while I draw the water milady? You can get punch or sour-sap or tamarind.

ANNIE: I'll just have coffee.

CHLOE: Yes milady.

ANNIE: You have children Chloe?

CHLOE: No milady. I want the right daddy for them, so they're high-brown with good hair. I don't want any nayga pickneys.

ANNIE: Nayga?

CHLOE: Niggers mam. There are niggers like Rhone, and there are mulattos like me. My father got away with cook and that was me, a mulatto. Mulattos come from white men with black women.

ANNIE: Or white women with black men.

CHLOE: What mam?

ANNIE: Black men with white women.

CHLOE: Never heard of it mam. No black man should risk that.

ANNIE: What would happen?

CHLOE: They would chop off his sinting.

ANNIE: *(Laughing at the pun.)* Sin-thing.

CHLOE: They would chop it off. Play with niggers they take liberties with you. Lie down in your bed with their fleas.

ANNIE: *(Looking to escape.)* Do they?

CHLOE: You hear what is happening in San Domingo? A little ugly black coachman named Toussaint slept with the white ladies and took over, and San Domingo's collapsed. All the pretty plantations are ruinate. You heard about it?

ANNIE: I hear about nothing else.

CHLOE: Aren't you frightened it will spread?

ANNIE: Slaves seldom rise. Too tired, too frightened, too uncertain whether the rebels aren't as insane as the tyrants.

CHLOE: You want sugar mam?

ANNIE: I'll use the honey.

CHLOE: You an abolitionist milady?

ANNIE: Why?

CHLOE: Not using sugar?

ANNIE: Oh dear no, Chloe. I'm sure there must be reasons for slaughtering blacks to make sugar, when bees make honey so successfully. Beside, where would we be without the money?

CHLOE: Milady married for money?

ANNIE: Dear Chloe, how can anyone marry for money, only to risk screaming to death nine months later in child-bed? It's not on.

CHLOE: Unless you're a witch milady, and mean to get rid of the child.

ANNIE: In England they drink gin, and jump off tables.

CHLOE: A witch will murder both husband and child.

ANNIE: I do believe murdering husbands to be a most ancient anti-conception. You're left with a flat belly and a great fortune.

CHLOE: Unless you hang.

ANNIE: It's too hot to burn people, isn't it Chloe? I'm in two minds whether to be dressed for the mosquitoes or naked for the heat.

CHLOE: *(Alarmed.)* Milady walks naked? *(ANNIE looks at her.)* I'll open the blinds in your rooms to let in the cool.

ANNIE: When does your master return?

CHLOE: He never says, milady.

ANNIE: Does he just arrive, or send word?

CHLOE: He arrives milady, or sends word.

She exits, and RHONE enters.

ANNIE: Fan me.

RHONE: There are boys to do that mam.

ANNIE looks at him.

You want a boy to fan you mam?

ANNIE: Coffee?

RHONE: I'm not high enough yet to sip coffee in the great-house milady.

ANNIE: *(Showing him some sketches.)* Look at these.

RHONE: Niggers.

ANNIE: Sailors on the boat.

RHONE puts down the sketch-book disdainfully.

RHONE: Such big thick lips.

ANNIE: Like yours.

Long silence.

RHONE: Far too ugly to mark down on paper.

ANNIE: Beautiful.

RHONE: What?

ANNIE: Your lips.

RHONE is silent. CHLOE knocks and enters.

CHLOE: Your scented bath's ready milady.

ANNIE: Thanks, my dear.

CHLOE exits and spies on them.

I've got a splinter in my foot. Take it out.

RHONE: There again you need a boy mam.

ANNIE: I'll get a needle.

RHONE: I've never touched a white lady, milady.

ANNIE: I want to sketch you.

RHONE: When?

ANNIE: When Chloe's fast asleep.

RHONE bows and exits. Lights on CHLOE in the courtyard, talking to ABUKU.

CHLOE: Ride hard, and tell bakkra to come back here tonight.

Lights on RHONE spreading his sleeping-mat on the drawing-room floor. He sits on the mat, troubled. CHLOE lights the candles. There's fierce drumming in the distance. Lights on ANNIE in her bedroom with LUCINDA. They're smoking herbs.

ANNIE: They're drumming the God over from Africa.

LUCINDA: Not permitted.

ANNIE: Call him from Africa.

LUCINDA: Not permitted.

ANNIE: God takes six hours to cross the sea.

LUCINDA: And when he come he not sea-sick...

ANNIE: Or weary.

LUCINDA: And he's so glad to see us...

ANNIE: He takes shape and form, like a man.

LUCINDA: And sit round the table and drink a rum and laugh and curse, and after he give us the news he pinch the ladies, and we curse him, yes.

ANNIE: Yes, but you're glad, because he's the bigger headman.

LUCINDA: Bigger than bakkra.

ANNIE: And he came far to see us, and we take him and grind him and possess him.

LUCINDA: And grab his back and shudder.

ANNIE: *(Dialect.)* And God sinting stand up well strong.

LUCINDA: And never go down.

ANNIE: Till he pleasure us.

LUCINDA: And free us.

ANNIE: And free us.

PALMER steals, unseen, into the dark drawing-room.

RHONE: *(Sitting on his mat, talking to himself.)* Man, you just promote. Walk and think twice. Walk and think three times. Tek a walk. *(He doesn't move.)*

PALMER, unseen watches him.

Upstairs, LUCINDA smoking, mutters to ANNIE.

LUCINDA: Rhone is murder.

ANNIE: Just what I need.

PALMER goes rigid as someone comes down the stairs. It turns out to be CHLOE. She looks in his direction but can't see him in the shadows, and goes off. RHONE puts out a few candles, then goes back to his mat and lies down. PALMER watches the stairs waiting for ANNIE to come down.

Upstairs ANNIE dolls herself up with powder and perfume. Downstairs PALMER's hands are sweating. He wipes them and shuts his eyes with anxiety.

ANNIE: *(To LUCINDA.)* Go down and put out the candles.

LUCINDA: Is Herrera's ghost in the house?

ANNIE: He's not.

LUCINDA: Did you call him?

ANNIE: He's frightened of Palmer.

LUCINDA: Mr. Palmer is not in the house.

ANNIE: He must be. Go and put out the candles.

RHONE looks up as LUCINDA comes down the stairs. She starts to put out the candles and sees PALMER.

PALMER: Where's milady?

LUCINDA: She can't sleep for the drums, so she asked me to sit with her.

PALMER goes upstairs.

ANNIE: *(To PALMER.)* You were quick.

PALMER: There's talk.

ANNIE: Mere talk never lost a good husband.

PALMER: Was I palmed off with a stable lad's shag?

ANNIE: Even stable-lads swell bellies Mr. Palmer, and I was flat as an angel.

PALMER: You were not intact.

ANNIE: I lost it, alas, on a horse.

PALMER: Was I a jackass to believe that?

ANNIE: My father told you, before the banns.

PALMER: There's talk of murder.

ANNIE: That was my great grand-mamma. She murdered her good husband in bed, and strangled the dumb bitch that barked at her.

PALMER: Is there insanity in your family?

ANNIE: She said there were more good men than good land. She was perfectly sane.

PALMER: Did she hang?

ANNIE: They hanged a servant. It was clearly a male job. She said there were too many servants.

PALMER: There's talk of witchcraft.

ANNIE: Witches are useless aren't they my dear. They couldn't even put out the fires that burned them. Come to bed.

PALMER: You break my heart and I'll break your neck.

PALMER exits. ANNIE stands at her window till she hears his horse gallop away, then she goes downstairs to RHONE, and bares a candle-lit breast.

ANNIE: You daren't tell, and I daren't tell.

RHONE: Right here quick.

ANNIE: Come to the sea, and swim in it.

RHONE: We can do everything right here quick.

ANNIE: I want to play. *(She strokes it with her toe.)*

RHONE: *(Drowning.)* I have my life. I have a woman.

ANNIE: She has black breasts, with purple nipples.

RHONE: *(Grabbing at her.)* Sea too far.

ANNIE: I'm a witch. Fly me.

RHONE: Don't tease me. Don't rape me.

ANNIE: You want me?

RHONE: Now.

ANNIE exits and RHONE pursues her.

Lights up on CHLOE clearing up coffee cups in the drawing-room. She starts to exit with a tray when ANNIE enters through the front door.

ANNIE: Chloe, come here. (*CHLOE puts tray down and walks the length of the room.)* Are you spying on me?

CHLOE: *(Raising her voice.)* Niggers are good for nothing but darkness and lechery. They have a big heavy black sinting like the devil, and lust burns the babies up. Bakkra give the women £5 for every pickney, but they not breedin'. They shrink from the pain God almighty ordain.

ANNIE: You want them to suffer, do you Chloe?

CHLOE: Woman tempted man with the apple of sex.

ANNIE: And she must suffer for it?

CHLOE: Yes mam. Woman ate the apple, and discovered sex, and lost all shame, and lift up her fig-leaf, and she must suffer the pains of hell. Monthly.

ANNIE: You won't spy on me again, will you Chloe?

CHLOE: *(Frightened.)* What are you doing to me?

ANNIE: Are you in pain?

CHLOE: My monthly is starting on me.

ANNIE: Is it your monthly?

CHLOE: It's early. *(Frantic.)* I need rum.

ANNIE: Can't you reach it?

CHLOE falls, heading for the rum.

CHLOE: *(Screaming.)* Don't witch me, I beg you, don't witch me.

ANNIE: You go to the witches, don't you?

CHLOE: *(Weeping.)* Yes mam.

ANNIE: Do they heal you?

CHLOE: No milady. They use herbs, and when herbs fail, they use charms, and I smell hell every month, but I don't know where else to turn. I want to breed for Cupid, but I can't. *(Weeps.)* I'm a mule.

ANNIE: For every malady of woman there's a leaf in the forest, and the wise women who searched for them for centuries to stop their own pain and enjoy their desires, were called witches and burnt, and their knowledge destroyed. I do fear that the sexually disturbed rule the world, working our bodies to exhaustion, making useless silver and sugar and gold, binding with briars our joys and desires, as Mr. Blake the poet said. And you spy for them.

CHLOE: Milady, I'm a slave. I love who I fear, and I fear you more than bakkra. My eyes are shut milady.

ANNIE: I'll have my bath now Chloe. That sounds delicious.

Both exit. Lights down to just before dawn. Night noises. Gunshots. CHLOE appears at the top of the stairs, listening to them. ANNIE and RHONE enter, naked, from the sea, and cross CHLOE on the stairs. She averts her eyes.

CHLOE: Morning milady.

ANNIE: Dare anyone enter my rooms?

CHLOE: No milady.

ANNIE: We are not to be disturbed.

CHLOE: I am only awake because I hear gun fire in the night.

ANNIE: Couldn't you sleep?

CHLOE: No milady.

ANNIE: Neither did we my dear. Goodnight Chloe.

Exits with RHONE. CHLOE kneels down and prays. We hear the wash of the beautiful Caribbean. DAWES quietly enters the drawing-room. Sees CHLOE praying. Takes a rum. Looks at RHONE's empty mat. Glances upstairs. Calls quietly to CHLOE, talking in whispers.

DAWES: S-s-s-t. During the night I ran into five runaways.

CHLOE: Did they have guns?

DAWES: No, and wanted mine. I fired twice. Three ran away. *(Drinks.)* Two less… When I kill I feel sentimental, and came to see you in the delicate hours. *(He looks again at*

RHONE's empty mat and starts sniffing, his nostrils flaring.) You smell anything in this house?

CHLOE: Like what?

DAWES: Passion.

CHLOE: There is no passion in this house.

DAWES: I smell pussy-juice.

CHLOE: You smell your own tail.

DAWES: Some men can smell water and I can smell passion. I smell carnality in the house.

CHLOE: Wine is a mocker.

DAWES: You think I am drunk.

CHLOE: Strong drink is ragin'.

DAWES: I sincerely hope I am drunk. I am carnal when drunk. You think the carnality I smell may be my own?

CHLOE: Yes Mr. Dawes.

DAWES: Anytime I hear the word carnal I get a feeling right here between the eyebrows. (*Touches his cock.*)

CHLOE: Yes me God.

DAWES: You feel carnal?

CHLOE: I have the house-work to do. *(Bed starts creaking.)*

DAWES: *(Listening.)* Hear me state my predicament.

CHLOE: *(Listening.)* State your predicament Mr. Dawes.

DAWES: My sinting got lazy, and want to sleep at night, and need sensual refinements to incite it.

CHLOE: *(Listening.)* Refinement?

DAWES: *(Listening.)* Refinement.

CHLOE: What about the white ladies? They not sensually refined?

DAWES: Pshaw, every nigger wants a white woman, because that is either revenge or promotion, but I don't need promotion.

CHLOE: And what about revengin' dem?

DAWES: I get a conscience. *(He gets excited by the creaking bed and starts feeling CHLOE.)*

CHLOE: Bakkra came back again in the night.

DAWES: I knew I smelt passion. The sound of the bed is very incitin'.

CHLOE: *(Fending him off.)* What about all the young coloured girls in the kitchen?

DAWES: Phsaw, they too renk and too young. They want romance and play the man not the ball.

CHLOE: Lawd, Mr. Dawes, state your requirement to every house-gal and one of them will know how to incite you.

DAWES: Chloe, is that now. I don't know exactly what I want. All I know is I go along without satisfaction, yet I am a big man on this estate. *(Dialect.)* Habbe, habbe, no want it. Want-it, want-it, can't get it.

CHLOE: You have it you don't want it, you want it, you want it, you can't get it.

DAWES: That's my predicament.

CHLOE: But you're a big side-man on the estate. You can get it anytime.

DAWES: But if I can get it, I don't want it. I'm chronic.

CHLOE: I hear unmentionable things about you Mr. Dawes. I hear you suffer from sadness after the act.

DAWES: There is nothing unmentionable about that.

CHLOE: The unmentionable, of course, cannot be mentioned.

The creaking stops. DAWES listens a long time, enjoining CHLOE to silence every so often. In the stillness RHONE appears at the top of the stairs. He hears and sees nobody and starts descending. CHLOE sees him and distracts DAWES.

(*Amorously.*) Come here Mr. Dawes.

RHONE reverses up the stairs.

DAWES: You want me now?

CHLOE: Well to tell you the God's truth Mr. Dawes I don't want you at all, but you can break down me door if that will incite you.

DAWES: That won't suit.

CHLOE: Well whatever suit you sir.

DAWES: Your tail must say yes, and your mouth must demurely say no.

CHLOE: My mouth say yes, and my tail say no.

DAWES: That is lip-service.

CHLOE: What more you want?

DAWES: Tails yes, heads no.

CHLOE: That's very refined.

DAWES: And I don't want anybody else down there but me. So talk now.

CHLOE: Yes Mr. Dawes, but right now it's me monthly.

DAWES: (*Disgusted.*) Oh me God. You know there are four swear words in the Jamaican language for your condition: rass-cloth, bumbo-cloth, blood-cloth, pussy-cloth. That must be unique.

CHLOE exits, shocked as ANNIE enters.

DAWES: Milady slept well?

ANNIE: And safely thank you Dawes.

DAWES: Is bakkra upstairs?

ANNIE: Why?

DAWES: Rhone slept in the house?

ANNIE: Yes.

DAWES: I trust not too soundly milady.

ANNIE: Sleep on a mat on the floor would hardly be sound.

They exit in different directions. PRINCESS enters with an armful of flowers and puts them in a vase. ANNIE re-enters with a cup of tea.

PRINCESS: *(Pouring a powder into the tea.)* Swallow this.

ANNIE: How many more?

PRINCESS: Two more milady. Dawes is spying on you.

ANNIE: Tell me about Dawes.

PRINCESS: He's a forger, and will forge the deeds for this house.

ANNIE: Tell me more.

PRINCESS: He has two eyes and one mouth and sees twice as much as he says.

ANNIE: I feel exposed.

PRINCESS: What will you do about Dawes?

ANNIE: Nothing. I never put my head out to see if I'm seen… Such an exquisite morning. So clear. And there's my headless man. He put his head out. *(PRINCESS sees nothing.)* Do you see spooks my dear?

PRINCESS: No milady.

ANNIE: The dogs chewed his head off. Can't you even sense him? Herrera. *(Rolls the name round her tongue.)* Mr. Herrera. What a torso. And there's his bleeding head. I have no idea how I'll get those two together... Yes, I think I know.

Blackout.

Lights up on PALMER in the drawing room, leafing through ANNIE's sketchbook. RHONE enters.

PALMER: She's sketching Abuku?

RHONE: Yes bakkra.

PALMER: She's sketching you?

RHONE: Yes, sir.

PALMER: *(Dismissing RHONE.)* That is all. Send Dawes in. *(RHONE exits. PALMER pours himself a rum.)*

Dawes...

DAWES: Bakkra.

PALMER: I want to look at my will.

DAWES: It can't be changed sir. Milady inherits. No strings.

PALMER: That is an incitement to murder.

DAWES: I warned you sir.

PALMER: Dawes.

DAWES: Bakkra?

PALMER: You forged the deed for the Ramble estate.

DAWES: And now Ramble is yours.

PALMER: Forge a new will. Milady inherits, unless I die childless or suspiciously. Then Cupid inherits. If the rumours are true it will not be contested.

DAWES: Your attorney must be party to that, and he's in England.

PALMER: He'll be back in a fortnight. On the next boat. I'll be on the estate if you want me.

Both exit. RHONE re-enters, looking for ANNIE. She comes in with flowers from the garden.

RHONE: There is suspicion.

ANNIE: Not too late to stop.

RHONE: Too late. *(He kisses her; romantic.)* Why are you married? Why did you marry?

ANNIE: My hole is my fortune. And now my husband means to kill me with child. Unless he dies.

RHONE: *(Dialect.)* Bakkra na dead. Bakkra born under the ram. Bakkra piss heavy.

ANNIE: I hear he prowls the estate at night, peeping into slave-huts.

RHONE: Yes.

ANNIE: A stone could brain him.

RHONE: Yes.

ANNIE: And there are runaways to blame.

RHONE: Yes.

ANNIE: You wouldn't dare, would you?

RHONE: What?

ANNIE: Murder him.

RHONE: No milady, you'd sell up and sail away.

ANNIE: Murder him and have your freedom.

RHONE: I want you.

ANNIE: I'll get you a rattle and you can play with that.

RHONE: You called me, milady.

ANNIE: That was Tuesday.

RHONE: Everyday is Tuesday now.

ANNIE: You weren't much cop anyway.

RHONE: You were laughin' and moanin'.

ANNIE: Oh, a little flattery does a man good. More good than it did me.

RHONE: You were moving up your belly.

ANNIE: I was panting after pleasure and not getting any.

RHONE hears a horse pull up, and exits.

PALMER: *(To ANNIE.)* I want the doctor to visit you.

ANNIE: What for?

PALMER: If you don't breed, Cupid inherits.

ANNIE: *(Casually.)* Is that in the settlement?

PALMER: The doctor will look to your interest. He's the most expensive man in the business.

ANNIE: My father was sober when he signed that?

PALMER: There's no law between us. The law between us is love. I'm going to stay at my estate in Falmouth.

PALMER exits. ANNIE goes upstairs, and ABUKU races in hunting mosquitoes, whooping, dancing, imitating their hum and singing as he kills them.

ABUKU: *(Singing.)* Mosquito one, mosquito two,
Mosquito taste nice with rice and callalou.

LUCINDA enters with a water-jar, followed by CHLOE in a new dress.

CHLOE: Lucinda I'm goin' to a dance with Cupid. You love me dress?

LUCINDA: And the hat.

CHLOE: You think it will stagger the crowd?

ABUKU: Lawd Miss Chloe, it loud, everybody will hear you.

CHLOE: I like to look good.

LUCINDA: That will razzle and dazzle the crowd Miss Chloe. Who givin' dance?

CHLOE: Barrett daughter. She want to hear all about Miss Annie so they invite me. Everybody want to hear about her, and the rumours, great God, what am I to say to be both loyal and truthful. I can't even tek a rum because there is a truth in rum, so I am sober as a judge. And I hear dogs all night and can't sleep, but don't tell bakkra, or he will sell me.

CUPID enters. CHLOE's face falls: He is not even dressed.

CUPID: Abuku, you rat-catcher you. *(Embraces him.)*

CHLOE: The Barrett gal is so faisty I want to look good. Plenty poor whites will be there, and the ugly Barrett gal wan to hook a white man, so she goin' to dance and rub till baby come, but over-exertion cause yellow fever and if they dead she can't marry dem. And lawd, I can't tek the conversation. They moan and groan and complain about the niggers, then they over-eat and get bilious and tek calomel. *(To ABUKU and LUCINDA.)* Come and help me get Miss Annie's tea. I am in haste. Cupid get dressed.

CHLOE exits with ABUKU and LUCINDA as ANNIE comes down and cuts off CUPID's exit.

ANNIE: Your father said I should talk to you. He didn't tell me what to say.

CUPID: You could offer me an estate or two.

ANNIE: The estates are your father's. You should inherit them.

CUPID: And where would that leave you milady?

ANNIE: You could offer me an estate or two.

CUPID: Or ditch you, like your husband ditches black women.

ANNIE: *(Tearing the head off a rose and getting pricked in the process.)* Like that?

CUPID: Milady actually bleeds.

ANNIE: *(Flirting.)* Beast, do attend me.

CUPID: Go and dip it in the salt-water milady. It's a sea of blood.

An African song drifts in from the garden.

ANNIE: What's he singing?

CUPID: The only thing worse than slavery is love.

ANNIE: *(As the song changes.)* And what's he singing now?

CUPID: The only thing worse than love is slavery.

CHLOE enters with tea.

ANNIE: Better play love, at your age.

CUPID: *(To CHLOE.)* Let's play love.

CHLOE: Waiting, watching for my love to come. Fearing what I see, in the cards. Reading the leaves. Go man go.

CUPID: That's very brief suffering.

CHLOE: I've suffered. It's your turn.

CUPID: Heart-ache without you. Kick my feet, hold my head, cry heart-ache…

RHONE re-enters, curious, hovering.

CHLOE: Cupid is taking me to a dance mam and he's later than women.

CUPID: Every minute I was late I missed you miss, I missed you.

CHLOE: I'm afraid of the runaways on the road.

CUPID: You want to hear a runaway song?

RHONE: Such songs may not be sung in the great-house milady.

ANNIE: Talk it then.

CUPID: White man come wid powder, come wid gun.
Nigger shiver, nigger shake, nigger stagger.
Nigger stagger, nigger stumble,
Nigger dead.

Dey come wid powder, come wid gun,
Poi poi,
Bu-dum,
And what happen bredda, what happen den?
Dead man get up and scare dem.
Dead man get up, and dead man scare dem.

RHONE: Bakkra says such things may not be said in the great-house milady.

ANNIE: Kindly leave.

RHONE bows and exits.

CUPID: You tell me a poem.

ANNIE: I went to the garden of love
And saw what I never had seen
A chapel was built in the midst
Where I used to play on the green
And the gates of this chapel were shut
And "thou shalt not" writ over the door
And priests in black gowns were walking their rounds
And binding with briars my joys and desires.

CUPID: You want to hear why the great African empires fell.

ANNIE: Tell me why the great African empires fell.

CUPID: Because men of action became men of opium. Kings with long pipes, smoking herbs to feel joy in their bodies. They liked feeling good. That's why they never made guns because they didn't like pain. They sat under shady trees, talking about psychic things: dreams, and death, and life everlasting. Then they ate and their bellies were full but their bodies felt empty, so they danced in a frenzy till they fell into a trance and out of this world. Africans are men with the dance on them, bred over centuries, and God punished them with fighting, fornicating white men, out there on business.

ANNIE: Our bellies are full, but our bodies are empty. Wonderful!

CUPID: Milady quotes me.

PRINCESS: *(Entering with buns.)* Chloe, the buns are burnt. I'm sorry. I'm sorry milady.

ANNIE: Sit down and have some tea, all of you.

CUPID: Chloe, you ever sat down in a great-house from the day you were born?

CHLOE: Surely I sit down. If milady say sit I sit down.

CUPID: No, no, I don't mean sit down in attendance to please milady. I mean enter and sit down on the Wedgwood to please your own bottom.

ANNIE laughs.

CHLOE: Is not Wedgwood it name. *(Dialect.)*

CUPID: What?

CHLOE: The chair.

CUPID: Yes, Wedgwood from England, or Chippendale. I forget. But that's what you slave for.

PRINCESS: *(A warning glance at CUPID.)* Chippendale.

CHLOE: I have my own room upstairs to sit down in. Why should I want to be sitting down here?

CUPID: But you ever sit down in the Chippendale?

CHLOE: Like a white lady?

CUPID: Of course not like a white lady. How could you sit down like a white lady. But I mean, when you were alone in the house, and nobody was looking, nobody at all, house totally empty, did you ever look round you and sit down. *(He wiggles his arse mockingly and sits luxuriously, crossing his legs.)* Easy. I used to read the news about Toussaint sitting on the floor. Do sit down Miss Chloe. *(CHLOE sits down uneasily, and gets up immediately. They all laugh. CUPID says in a posh English accent.)* Do sit at least on the edge of the seat.

CHLOE: He'll die laughing at me.

CUPID: Nine nights after my death there will be dancing and merriment.

ANNIE: He seems to be dying in earnest.

PRINCESS: *(Level voice.)* He spends his life in his head, dying in rebellions.

ANNIE: It's the only way to stay alive.

PRINCESS: Without dignity.

CUPID, humiliated, leaves, and CHLOE follows to comfort him. PRINCESS sprinkles another powder-dose in ANNIE's tea.

ANNIE: I feel wretches pulling at my insides. Nothing else.

PRINCESS: You don't show it.

ANNIE: I feel wretched.

PRINCESS: You'll soon be flat, and your husband demented.

ANNIE: *(Of work songs in the distance.)* Why are they singing?

PRINCESS: They're digging the new shit-pit.

ANNIE: *(Despairing of powders.)* I'm going for a ride. The horse might kick me.

PRINCESS: You go and lie down.

ANNIE: For nine months? Times twelve children? Tied like a beast to a stick? My mother sat sick on a couch all her life, and dropped twelve, like a sow... Distract me my dear. Tell me about your time in England.

PRINCESS: I first heard about abolition in England, and stood there in those white drawing-rooms, saying how well off black people were.

ANNIE: You loved Palmer?

PRINCESS: When it was over I handed him a machete and said "Finish me."

ANNIE: That story pays for all your sins.

PRINCESS: I never had common-sense. My life blew me about. Some people are born sure-footed, not me.

ANNIE: They put one foot in front of the other like Dawes, and never fall off. See with brutal clarity in front of their nose.

PRINCESS: *(Laughing.)* They made me keeper of the vineyards. But my own vineyard have I not kept.

ANNIE: Talking of grapes, I fancy Cupid.

PRINCESS: White ladies are not Cupid's pleasure, milady.

ANNIE: I need love, and he seems a lovely likely boy. Not to be snared at.

PRINCESS: *(Alarmed.)* Nor easily snared.

ANNIE: He's nearer our colour than yours, m'dear.

PRINCESS: Cupid is no bed-slave milady.

ANNIE: Indeed not. If I'm childless he might inherit.

PRINCESS: I have no wish for Cupid to inherit.

ANNIE: I thought you were as anxious as I am to get rid of Palmer and his heirs.

PRINCESS: For the people. For freedom.

ANNIE: When does it come? The slave ships have sailed for a million years, and every other year there is rebellion, put down by ghouls and blood-bats with relish. There's a cold rage that burns in their loins and licks at their brain, and only blood puts it out. You can't wish Cupid to be mutilated in some passing rebellion.

PRINCESS: If you are what you are, you must be for freedom.

ANNIE: When freedom comes there will be a man with a gun on every street-corner, and the dungeons will be so full men will sleep standing up. Freedom takes a year to come and stays a day. Freedom lasts too long.

PRINCESS: The people are rising. Freedom is nigh.

ANNIE: My dear, look at me. I have a pretty painted face. Dollars in my head. My eyes are two golden guineas, my mouth blindly consumes. I am people. Who are you? A doomed angry fool. I'd rather stew in Palmer's bed and breed vermin. I'd rather go riding than bleed for the world. I'm going riding.

PRINCESS: Killers like Dawes and Rhone will protect you.

ANNIE: I pray they do. The world's a great-house. A few eat at table, and many wait on them.

PRINCESS: That's history. That's dead.

ANNIE: That's past, present and future.

PRINCESS: Slavery will burn.

PRINCESS exits as RHONE, hovering, enters.

RHONE: I am content to walk only after white men. Bakkra tread first, then I tread. Nobody else.

ANNIE: *(Howling.)* I'm locked in sin with this jealous fool. What's the good of sin, if we're locked in.

RHONE: Fix time and place to meet, so I don't wait and fret.

ANNIE: Go to your woman tonight, and tomorrow come and gentle me.

RHONE: You tonight and she tomorrow night. No you tonight, and you tomorrow night.

He grabs her.

ANNIE: That hurts.

RHONE: You beast Cupid and bakkra will know.

ANNIE: I'll grind him under your nose. I'll sweat in his heat and stain his bed and make you smell hell, you stinking slave. *(Exit.)*

RHONE: Let bakkra hang me.

RHONE walks down the stairs and runs into DAWES.

DAWES: How is milady? All legs?

RHONE: Sir?

DAWES: You lost your tongue in her?

RHONE: What sir?

DAWES: Poor bakkra.

RHONE: I am in your debt for my promotion Mr. Dawes.

DAWES: So is bakkra in mine for various favours, and I fear it Rhone. A word to his fat fed safe-niggers and I am manure. I need my own men among them. They must be fed, armed and watered from the stores and that is why you are in charge. You must have wondered... The keys... *(He takes them.)* And when you find your tongue hold it, for the silver we lift must be melted.

RHONE: By me?

DAWES: Milady trusted you man. So do I.

RHONE: Milady?

DAWES: Dougall the mulatto militiaman in Montego Bay will melt the silver. See to it.

RHONE: *(Rattled.)* Bakkra will count the stores, and silver will not be found, and he will find I am sleeping with his wife.

DAWES: Is evidence for that in the stores?

RHONE: We'll be dead Mr. Dawes.

DAWES: We'll walk over their five estates, and into five great-houses, and there will be white flesh on white sheets in my bed. No man on this island will be richer than me. They dive into quick-sand for gain, but they won't be rich like me. God's blood, you mind the stores and we'll buy the safe-niggers, and three coffins for Palmer, his bitch and his bastard.

CHLOE: *(Off, screaming.)* Mr. Rhone, Mr. Dawes! *(Enters, running.)* Joko dead. Bakkra prize-nigger. Joko capture Herrera, and Joko dead. Herrera is haunting the estate.

DAWES: Ghosts frighten niggers.

CHLOE: I made bakkra sell Lucinda's children, and they are Herrera's and he's come back for me.

DAWES: Ghosts are harmless.

CHLOE: Is you, bakkra and Rhone murder him Mr. Dawes.

RHONE: Belief kill and cure, and bakkra don't believe, and I, Rhone, keeper of the stores, don't believe. *(Exit.)*

CHLOE: I am not staying in this house. Things are coming to pass. *(Exit.)*

DAWES helps himself to rum, listens to work-song as slaves dig shit-pit, and exits.

Lights down. PALMER arrives home.

PALMER: I am here again.

RHONE: *(Off.)* Safe and sound. Bakkra come.

The cry "Bakkra come" echoes round the estate. RHONE enters, then DAWES.

PALMER: You look after my wife?

RHONE: And your stores.

PALMER: Where are you going?

RHONE: To grease your boots.

RHONE exits.

DAWES: Tall rum?

PALMER: You get the invites for Lady Nugent's ball?

DAWES: Yes bakkra.

PALMER: *(Shouts.)* Miss Annie… But Dawes, I passed a little gal with new breasts washing herself in the river. I slid down the slope, the gal ran and fought like a bush-dog, but I get me hand up and work her and wet her, and when I took her I knew I'd come home. The gal pussy purple, her belly fit, soon she drop a pickney for me. Yes Dawes, now I'm home again. Sink another rum. *(Shouts.)* Miss Annie! I hear Mitchell's son getting 600 hogshead of sugar this year.

DAWES: Well bakkra, still all in all he's not rich like you. And his wife looks like the bull from Lacovia.

PALMER: But 600. Me, 500.

DAWES: Bakkra, look on the class of sulky you drive, and look on the sulky Mitchell drives. Mitchell can't argue with you.

PALMER: I'm glad to come home and put up me foot. Let breeze blow my balls. So who's dead and who's still sweating?

DAWES: Bakkra… your best prize-nigger's gone.

PALMER: Joko?

DAWES: Joko capture Herrera and Joko dead.

PALMER: How?

DAWES: His hand get ketch in the mill.

PALMER: You didn't sever the limb?

DAWES: Four of them stand up feeding cane, and Joko's hand ketch.

PALMER: And not one of them grabbed the hatchet and chopped it off.

DAWES: So the whole of Joko gone.

PALMER: The hatchet is right there, for that very purpose, and you never used it.

DAWES: The mill sucked him in, and grind him up with the cane.

PALMER: It's the first prize-nigger I've ever lost.

DAWES: Worth 200 pounds.

PALMER: How his hand ketch?

DAWES: They say he was dozing, and they complain about the hours, they say Kelly worked 'em over the twelve hours and up to fifteen. But fifteen is nutten to Joko. Joko work from sun to moon in the mill-house, two weeks straight. Cane lice, hours, nutten stop him.

PALMER: *(Drinking.)* Joko's blood mek good rum.

DAWES: Niggers are singing that Joko's blood shed for freedom.

PALMER: Where is Chloe?

DAWES: Bakkra the word in every mouth is that Herrera push Joko.

PALMER: Where is Chloe?

DAWES: She is stoopin' down in the yard and won't move.

PALMER runs out to CHLOE who is being tended by ABUKU.

CHLOE: I made you sell Lucinda's children Mr. Palmer and one of them was Herrera's.

PALMER: If there is fear in the great-house it will be heard all over the estate. Get up.

ABUKU: *(Trying to feed her.)* You must eat, Miss Chloe.

PALMER: White people fear men more than monsters. That is why we are successful on earth and niggers are successful in heaven.

CHLOE: I want to sleep.

ABUKU: Eat up Miss Chloe.

CHLOE: Put out food for Herrera.

PALMER: Herrera is dead. Get up or go back to the blasted slave-gang. Get up! *(He gives her a helluva beating and kicking. She doesn't cry or move.)*

Dawes, send her back to the slave-gang.

Lights up in ANNIE's room. She talks to LUCINDA and plaits her hair.

LUCINDA: Here's a book to pass the time till the powder works.

ANNIE: What's it about.

LUCINDA: A lady who pleasured her slaves, and murdered them and her husband by witchcraft.

ANNIE: I trust it has a happy ending.

LUCINDA: No. Bakkra will beat you black and blue, then lock you up till you breed.

ANNIE: He won't live long enough.

LUCINDA: Then Cupid inherits and you marry him. Happy ending.

ANNIE: I fear for Cupid's pain and death. I reek and sizzle with fear for him.

LUCINDA: His mother fears you.

ANNIE: She's a martyr. I'm a murderer.

LUCINDA: Is there something murderous about women in your family?

ANNIE: It frightens me. I became a woman at twelve, and started seeing the dead walk. My servant said she had to fuck the devil out of me, and so she did it for years, and held it over me when I wished to marry. So I set her alight. I do fear there's more rage than love.

LUCINDA: *(With sympathy.)* Yes milady.

ANNIE: I put you in danger. Go back to the kitchen.

LUCINDA: You'll say you didn't like me?

ANNIE: Stroke my feet for the last time. *(LUCINDA strokes her feet.)* More, more.

LUCINDA: Greedy pig.

ANNIE: Now go back to the kitchen.

LUCINDA: *(Refusing.)* I'm so glad Herrera's alive, I wouldn't mind joining him.

ANNIE: *(Listening to her belly.)* But that's not the big news…

LUCINDA: You're well again?

ANNIE: *(Dancing.)* Yes. Yes. Yes.

Lights down.

PALMER enters the drawing-room.

PALMER: *(Shouting.)* Milady!

ANNIE comes downstairs.

ANNIE: My lord.

PALMER: You never dress up for me. *(He holds her.)* For a man like me you undress.

ANNIE: Oh you can't. I've bled.

PALMER: You've lost my baby again?

ANNIE: You grind me too keenly.

PALMER: But not for a week.

ANNIE: It's unnatural at this time grinding at all.

PALMER: Jesus Christ. I heard you rode all over the parish.

ANNIE: Only on the estate.

PALMER: You didn't hear me tell you to stay in the house. *(Whips her several times with his riding-whip.)* You think I went clear to England for a mule?

ANNIE: No, clearly you went for a breeding slave.

PALMER: They'll pull twelve children from your belly, and number one will start now. I'm going to man you and breed you and lock you up for nine months till you drop, and nine months after that, one a year, till my quiver's full. So help me God. *(He drags her up the stairs.)*

Act Two

SCENE ONE

Next day. A hellish noise offstage of servants squealing and pans dropping. ABUKU, the rat-catcher, runs in chasing rats. He shows ANNIE three dead rats.

ANNIE: They look like men. Who are they?

ABUKU: Rats milady.

ANNIE: This white one is bakkra, this brown one is Dawes, and who is this one?

ABUKU: This black one is Mister Rhone.

ANNIE: This one had worms, this one lost his head, and this one had fever and his eyes fell out. What shall we do with em?

ABUKU: Bury dem.

ANNIE: Bury dem, bury dem,
    Bury the three of 'em,
    Bury dem, bury dem,
    Hell will be rid of 'em.

ABUKU exits. ANNIE dances.

Where I can't witch dem I'll guile 'em,
    And gull 'em,
    And prey on their endless sexual fears,
    And bury dem.

PALMER: *(Entering.)* No dancing Miss Annie. No gallivantin'. Lie down in the sun and get black. Get the servants to rub fat on your back and stroke your foot-bottom. And I will come and kiss you all over.

ANNIE: Shall we visit our neighbours?

PALMER: *(Mocking the neighbours' questions.)* "And how is England, and how is Jamaica, and how is the weather?"

ANNIE: *(Laughing.)* Good wholesome questions.

PALMER: You want to get out of the house.

ANNIE: I'll go down to the mill and watch the work. Whatever do they think about while they're slaving?

PALMER: Love, money, liquor, tobacco and food. What else?

ANNIE: And being whipped would you think?

PALMER: *(Laughing.)* A reproach most ably contrived. Are you all black and blue? I'll tickle you pink. *(Tickles her.)*

ANNIE: *(Helpless with laughter; screaming.)* I'm sore. Struth no, Mr. Palmer.

PALMER: I'll take you tomorrow to the races.

ANNIE: I'll go with Cupid.

PALMER: Why?

ANNIE: Then there'll be no constraint on my purse, nor check on my wagers.

PALMER: *(Indirect apology.)* My father whipped my mother but once, and never had to again.

ANNIE: Was he a brute as well?

PALMER: And she was a saint. She grandmothered Cupid through fever and flux. Gave him cocoa-cream. Saved his life. Begged for his freedom.

ANNIE: Was she abolitionist?

PALMER: Oh Miss Annie, I never know when you mock me. Are your days empty?

ANNIE: Oh perfectly.

PALMER: You miss England? The painters, wits, poets.

ANNIE: Good God no. I'm a country girl. I hear cook complain to Lucinda about her inamorato and there's my literature. *(Jamaican accent.)* Lawd Lucinda, says cook, man's tail is too disorderly, and when I rudeness dem I love dem and wrap up in dem, can't walk me own road, weak, like sickness. This pretty nayga say he love me, and I decide to cover him with me glory, and let him into me glory-hole, and from then I don't see him. But don't bother wid heartache, says Lucinda, it's not strictly necessary.

PALMER roars.

PALMER: The accent, Lawd.

DAWES enters.

ANNIE: My mare needs a shoe. I shall see to her.

PALMER: But no riding, no dancing, no gallivantin'. It's not strictly necessary.

Exit ANNIE.

DAWES: Bakkra, Bea found this letter in milady's room.

PALMER: Did she read it?

DAWES: No sir.

PALMER: Did you?

DAWES: It is private bakkra.

PALMER: How do you know it's private?

DAWES: I read it bakkra.

PALMER: *(Reads aloud.)* "Dear Mother. I had Palmer for over two months on that boat boarding me five times a day. I tell him his mouth's raw, he jumps out of bed, chews stick for two minutes, there's a thick froth all over his gob, he wipes it off with his hand, wipes that on the linen. Holy God what have we to put up with simply to eat!"

Silence. PALMER sits down. Rent with anger. Walks around. Sits. Groans.

DAWES: Sink a rum sir. Settle your liver.

No answer. DAWES withdraws. PALMER knocks back two long rums. His breath gets short. He sits, reaching for breath. DAWES re-enters.

PALMER: It is revenge for the beating.

DAWES: And but a feeble revenge.

PALMER: She left it there for all and sundry to read.

DAWES: It is mere sulk and pique bakkra. Not serious. These are words.

PALMER: You fear worse? You fear harm?

DAWES: Yes sir.

PALMER: Physical harm?

DAWES: And material, yes sir, and madness above all.

PALMER: *(Hardly able to breathe.)* There could be harm greater than losing her? Losing so soon whatever love my wealth did command. I say my wealth. Or fearing it commanded nothing.

DAWES: Milady is a scorpio sir. Every torment done to a turn. They walk a tight rope. Play the leeways to a whisker, and work every bolt-hole.

PALMER: When we met she gazed at me Dawes. We lay a-bed gazing.

DAWES: Bakkra, gazing shouldn't be overlong. It delivers less than it promises, and may sour in a week. And you never can tell what they're gazing at. She gazed at five estates. You gazed at her.

PALMER: You see Dawes, she is not a black woman. I wouldn't tell everybody this, but between the sheets it f-f-f-f-t. Gone.

DAWES: You lose it?

PALMER: Too soon, too often. It's like cane-juice goin' to waste. All over the goddam bed. On her belly. On her belly. On me. I wipe it off and put it where it belongs, and mount again and again before I am ready, and she laughs at me with disdain and satisfaction. You have any such experience with women?

DAWES: When you start losin' them, you start lovin' them, and get weak and jealous. Now the black women, you fuck them like a captain sir. They get weak with love. Hang on to you. Naked, without pretence.

PALMER: Dawes, send for Dr. Baillie. I want him to look at her.

DAWES: I don't think she believes in doctors, your honour.

PALMER: Send for Baillie.

DAWES exits as ANNIE re-enters.

PALMER: Miss Annie I am down in the slave-yard if anybody wants me.

ANNIE: I'll bathe in the sun. *(Exits upstairs.)*

PALMER exits with DAWES. ANNIE sunbathes. CUPID enters her room by the backstairs.

CUPID: Where's my mother?

ANNIE: No one's here. Silence. As if they've gone to church.

CUPID: That's how I'll remember this house. People talking in glances and whispers.

ANNIE: Your father shouting in a house full of glances and whispers.

CUPID: If I can see that selling people is wrong, why can't he?

ANNIE: Men are, of all beasts, the most brutish, and your father among the more brutish of men.

CUPID: Yet it would be harder for me to leave this house than for a snail to crawl from its slimy, comfortable shell. I'm too fat, too spoilt, too blind, and knives must gut me till I'm lean and trim, and smoke and fire preserve me.

ANNIE: I like you very much as you are, though you sound very solemn.

CUPID: I spent the day among runaways.

ANNIE: They didn't cut your throat?

CUPID: They are tragic men, bound in all manhood and nature to fight, yet certain to die. So much fighting. So little freedom. Maybe you can't fight for freedom. Maybe the two have nothing to do with each other. Like storks and babies. Maybe only brutes win fights, and so fighting merely keeps brutes in power.

ANNIE: Will you join the runaways?

CUPID: My mother's question.

ANNIE: What do they want?

CUPID: The good flat land your five estates are on.

ANNIE: What would they want with them?

CUPID: Dig up the cane and plant food to eat. Not to sell.

ANNIE: Subsistence.

CUPID: No, their bellies are a steady market, not erratic, so if they can organise feeding themselves, *then* they can organise cash-crops like sugar for export. We do it the other way round and starve.

ANNIE: The estates are your father's.

CUPID: That's why they fight.

ANNIE: Are they ready to die?

CUPID: I live in the deep hell of yes and no and yes again.
   I fear pain, gaol and gaolers. Torture seems… I'm afraid
   bakkra will catch me and hang me.

ANNIE: You want to save the world.

CUPID: If I am worthy.

ANNIE: How do we become worthy?

CUPID: Abstain. Like Christ and St. Paul. Avoid women and
   self-abuse. Every night I pray, give me a clean heart oh
   God, so I may be worthy to turn this wicked world upside
   down.

He glances at her body.

ANNIE: *(Noting the glance.)* Did you come to see me or your
   mother?

CUPID: *(In a tremble.)* I was looking for my mother.

ANNIE: Do you hate women?

CUPID: Lust conceals hate.

ANNIE: Because it is made a sin, even in the innocent crib,
   and laden with guilt. The only love children get is platonic,
   although they can't breed.

CUPID: Why is it made a sin?

ANNIE: To change our nature. Make us cruel. Soldiers, not
   lovers. War follows peace, and peace is arming for war.
   Even sex is often the elation of conquest, if there *is* any
   elation. Our quick flesh can be as dead as India rubber.

CUPID: Milady dwells on the flesh.

ANNIE: What could be more central? Why isn't it dwelt
   on? Even our orgies and our lechery are disappointing,
   blighted, like Mr. Blake's rose. D'you know that poem?

   "Oh rose thou art sick,
   The invisible worm

That flies in the night, in the howling storm
Hath found out thy bed of crimson joy
And his dark secret love
Doth thy life destroy."

CUPID: I like the bed of crimson joy.

ANNIE: Oh Cupid, if flesh is evil isn't it easier to stick bayonets through men's bodies so only their souls need saving?

CUPID: So what shall we do to be saved?

ANNIE: Turn these five great-houses into schools, and bring children back to their senses. They can't even love their parents. Leave home and feel guilty about never seeing them. Then set up in marriage. There ought to be a Royal society for the protection of sensual children. Shall we join?

CUPID: They'd take us away in strait-jackets.

ANNIE: *(Laughing.)* Yes. Unless we convert men to Satan. He's the fallen angel of love, driven from heaven by a sexless God. Failing that, fill your pocket.

CUPID: With but a little persuasion you would make me a pagan.

ANNIE: Witches have fought for centuries for carnal insurrection. There is no other revolt worth dying for. Your mother believes in that felicity politicians speak of. I do not.

CUPID: My mother's a hero.

ANNIE: Heroes are so few they don't count. I want you alive.

CUPID: *(Laughing.)* Living within milady's India rubber legs.

ANNIE: *(Laughing.)* And in her possessive arms.

They hug. CUPID breaks off, runs downstairs where he finds his mother.

CUPID: How is Sammy?

PRINCESS: For sale.

CUPID: Slaves outnumber slavers ten to one. Let slaves end slavery. I'm a free man. *(PRINCESS slaps him.)* The rebels will end up slaving for their general.

PRINCESS: The rebels don't have a general.

CUPID: Is he a field-marshal?

PRINCESS: He's only a colonel.

CUPID: He'll be an emperor yet. Like Henri Christophe.

PRINCESS: That's what she told you?

CUPID: Slavery will be followed by wage-slavery. Wretches working day and night for a pittance.

PRINCESS: Wage slaves are not chained or branded or sold.

CUPID: Mamma, the greater part of the world will always hunger and thirst. And poverty will always plenty.

PRINCESS: You'll lay down your life lying with her?

CUPID: And she with me.

PRINCESS: Palmer's sent for the doctor to cut her. Maybe they'll make one thing and cut you.

Exit leaving CUPID stunned. He races upstairs to ANNIE and we see them listening as DAWES brings in PALMER and the doctor.

PALMER: She conceives easily, doc, but she can't hold the child. I believe she deliberately miscarries.

DOCTOR: She must rest. Sedentary pastimes. Sketching, knitting, light reading. There's a fixed amount of energy in the body, and the budding womb needs it all. Any vigorous movement takes energy from the foetus and its growth.

PALMER: Any vigorous movement?

DOCTOR: Any vigorous movement.

PALMER: Any vigorous movement at all?

DOCTOR: Any vigorous movement at all.

PALMER: At all, at all?

DOCTOR: Well, of course, your marital duties, your manly functions, but that's your movement, not hers. Does she lie still? She lies still, does she not?

PALMER: She thrashes about.

DOCTOR: Isn't she a lady?

PALMER: She's high, yes, the highest. But she wriggles her pelvis. Excuse the language.

DOCTOR: She has pleasure in it?

PALMER: Yes doc. You mustn't ask me again.

DOCTOR: But, speaking medically, does she actually enjoy it?

PALMER: Yes doc.

DOCTOR: Even revel in it?

PALMER: Yes, doc.

DOCTOR: You should have a word with the bishop. This may be wickedness. Pleasure is not part of the divine prescription. See to it she lies perfectly still, with her eyes shut. And lots of sketching. Light reading. No serious pursuits of any kind, save household duties. She should live, in fact, like an invalid.

PALMER: But the negresses hoe and weed till the day they drop.

DOCTOR: They are animal.

PALMER: They drop like goat-shit, Jesus Christ, nothing can shake 'em. What's wrong with her?

DOCTOR: The man who does not know sick women does not know women. Perpetual infirmities. Of every ten women who conceive, one will die, and two or three more disabled. How are her nerves?

PALMER: Very good.

DOCTOR: And in your opinion she actually enjoys it?

PALMER: You steer back to that again?

DOCTOR: It may of course be that she's suffering from an inflammation of the womb.

PALMER: You can handle that?

DOCTOR: Yes oh yes. You bruise the groin till there are blisters and sores, and they draw the inflammation from the womb to themselves; but for ladies well born, leeches might be less painful, applied to the breasts or outer lips of the genitals before the period is expected. Leeching is of course more expensive than blistering.

PALMER: We'd have to tie her down. She doesn't believe in those things.

DOCTOR: But her lust is disturbing in a lady. I'll look at her clitoris. Unnatural growth of the clitoris is likely to lead to immorality as well as serious disease.

PALMER: Immorality?

DOCTOR: Gross immorality if the clitoris is long. The longer, the grosser.

PALMER: Immorality.

DOCTOR: Amputation may be necessary.

PALMER goes silent.

I hear rumours infernal.

PALMER: You believe in such things?

DOCTOR: Witches have conspired in bed against us from the days of Eve and the snake. They can't breed, so there is no check on their lewdness, and only God knows who they mark. They know it's the rebellion we fear most, and they practice it to wreck our happiness, and our empire over them. Sex and witchcraft is one word. The only cure is to castrate her.

PALMER: I hate deformities.

DOCTOR: You won't see a thing.

PALMER: What would she be without her clitoris?

DOCTOR: Your happy, high-born, obedient wife.

PALMER: Surgery is wonderful.

DOCTOR: The devil in her will die, with her desires.

PALMER: Then cut her.

DOCTOR: Drug her food tonight. I'll come in the morning.

As DOCTOR exits, DAWES re-enters.

DAWES: What the doc say?

PALMER: Cut her.

DAWES: *(Slapping his thigh with excitement.)* Drug her food?

PALMER: Not tonight. I want to climb that mountain one more time.

DAWES: You want everything down there! You buy the whole hog!

PALMER: I saw this bitch of a stone in Montego Bay. A precious stone. It will sweeten her. I'll buy it Dawes. Tell her I'll be back by nightfall. I'm too often away from home.

DAWES sees PALMER out. Lights on ANNIE and CUPID upstairs listening.

ANNIE: *(To CUPID.)* You're sweating.

She wipes his sweat off and licks her hand. Then licks his face, and he avidly feels her. They exit by the backstairs for a fuck in the bush.

RHONE enters the drawing-room as LUCINDA comes down the stairs.

RHONE: Where is milady?

LUCINDA: Gone out with Cupid.

RHONE: When is bakkra comin' back?

LUCINDA: You goin' to tell?

He stands there breathing. Desperate. She exits as DAWES re-enters.

DAWES: For a walking prick you do flap.

RHONE: Bakkra will have to hang me Mr. Dawes.

DAWES: He'll put Sammy back in the stores, and Sammy can count. Why you want him to punish you?

RHONE: Niggers get caught by their prick. My life's finished.

DAWES: Bakkra is going to cut her, boy, and she will be flat white flab. She can't run from that, she can't hide, and you won't even want her. We're well set and if you crash, I'll split your dick, so don't crash.

Lights on ANNIE and CUPID re-entering bedroom by back-stairs.

CUPID: Read us our future.

ANNIE: Hush.

CUPID: Will we die?

ANNIE: They kill, we die.

CUPID: Is ecstasy rare?

ANNIE: Yes.

CUPID: I feel it now.

ANNIE: I'd walk bare-foot, bare-arsed, bare-back, breed, live and die for you.

CUPID: Why do you love me?

ANNIE: Because I can quote you.

CUPID: Why do I love you?

ANNIE: Because you have a nose for dark truth.

CUPID: I feel sweetly sad.

ANNIE: Moonchild.

CUPID: I must go and look after Sammy.

ANNIE: Is he ill?

CUPID: Yes.

ANNIE: Worried how slavery's getting on without him?

CUPID: And my mother's at a meeting.

ANNIE: Rebellion?

CUPID: I dread leaving you defenceless in this house.

ANNIE: I'm not defenceless… Wear this devil's cloth to keep out the dew.

CUPID runs, then turns back.

CUPID: *(Whispering.)* Tomorrow.

ANNIE: Tomorrow… I'll walk home with you.

Both exit.

Lights down to late afternoon. PALMER enters drawing-room with DAWES.

PALMER: I bought her a bitch of a diamond. Look at it Dawes.

DAWES: Pure light bakkra. The pure light of heaven.

PALMER: *(Shouting.)* Miss Annie… *(To DAWES, of the diamond.)* It will hang as heavy as my right ball. *(Shouts.)* Miss Annie!

DAWES, out of the corner of his eye, sees RHONE hovering.

DAWES: *(To RHONE.)* Go and find milady.

RHONE: Bakkra, I carry news for you.

PALMER: Where is she?

RHONE: Walking with Cupid sir.

PALMER: Go and find her.

RHONE: Bakkra…

DAWES: *(Cutting in.)* Go and find Mrs. Palmer.

RHONE stands there.

PALMER: *(Screams.)* Go!…

RHONE exits.

(To DAWES.) What is he telling me?

Before DAWES can answer, ANNIE enters. DAWES exits.

Where were you?

ANNIE: I open my legs. Need I open my mouth as well?

PALMER: I came back to say I'm sorry I hit you.

ANNIE: And sorry you raped me, and sorry you brag to Dawes about raping black girls. And sent for the doctor to cut me.

PALMER: You heard that?

ANNIE: *(Dry.)* Rhone my lover told me in bed.

PALMER: It took me a numb second to see the jest. My gut turned over. Turned black. No woman ever made me feel that. I bought you a stone as rare as you. We'll set it here in Jamaica and cut it. There are as good cutters and setters here in Jamaica as in England... My father couldn't buy this. Not this. Couldn't afford this. But with money so debased it'll be worth twice as much as I pay for it.

ANNIE: I've never seen a stone this size. Not even in England.

PALMER: Since God has made us rich, let us enjoy it.

ANNIE: Is it a present for castrating me?

PALMER: Who said that?

ANNIE: How many slaves died you think, mining this?

PALMER: *(Screaming.)* What are you? The French Revolution?!

ANNIE: You bought it, did you not, on approval? Give it back.

PALMER: It cost the earth. It made the friggin' Jew laugh under his cap. There I was, he thought, panderin' to my new bitch of a wife.

ANNIE: Take it away. I'll be on the bed with my drawers down and my knees up.

PALMER: Why did you marry me?

ANNIE: The better to murder you!

Exit ANNIE.

PALMER: *(Shouting.)* Dawes! Dawes!

DAWES enters.

I'll sleep at my neighbour's for safety. And speak to Rhone in the morning.

Both exit.

Lights down to night. RHONE spreads his mat on drawing-room floor. DAWES enters.

DAWES: There is peace in rum, take some. *(Pours him a drink.)*

RHONE: *(Declines drink.)* I am dead Mr. Dawes.

DAWES tosses off the drink and pours him another.

DAWES: Take more.

RHONE declines.

(Swallowing RHONE's drink.) There, that should make you feel better.

DAWES stabs RHONE, who stumbles off. DAWES follows and kills him.

Drawing-room. Dawn.
PALMER comes home from neighbour's. DAWES hails Caesar.

DAWES: When bakkra come everything settle, everything in order. When bakkra come down from Ramble, come back from the bay. One hundred estates fall in Jamaica, but not one belong to bakkra. Bakkra's five estates grind out 2,000 hogshead, and piss don't flow like bakkra's rum. Drought come, flood come, God reign and bakkra under God. Bakkra reign like a white sun and moon over five estates, like a white sun and moon bakkra shine. When bakkra stamp his foot, niggers hide. He is the honourable bakkra. Come bakkra and save Jamaica from witchcraft and the peril of Santo Domingo.

PALMER: I want no more reports about witchcraft! Never again!

DAWES: Bakkra, the whole estate says it's Herrera.

PALMER: I do not believe it.

DAWES: Then it cannot be true sir.

PALMER: You killed Rhone?

DAWES: Bakkra, who wanted revenge? Who wanted Sammy restored to pride and position? Cupid and Princess and Sammy himself. They want Sammy back in the stores to feed rebellion.

PALMER: Who killed him?

DAWES: Cupid planted a knife in his head. And the one blow served his mother and Sammy.

PALMER: You speak advisedly?

DAWES: I checked the stores. Silver is missing. Weapons are missing. Sammy was plundering for Princess, Cupid and rebellion.

PALMER: You have proof?

DAWES: Bakkra I captured two runaways who said Princess is in rebellion, and gave your slaves powders to abort. I can't find Cupid, we are chasing him and milady, but I arrest Princess and Sammy.

PALMER: She gave my wife powders?

DAWES: That might not be true, but it sound reasonable.

PALMER: Summon them. Sammy first.

DAWES leads in SAMMY.

SAMMY: Morning bakkra, and respect sir.

PALMER: You hear Rhone is dead?

SAMMY: Yes bakkra.

PALMER: Murdered by person or persons unknown.

SAMMY: Yes bakkra, I hear and I grieve.

PALMER: You felt grievance against him?

SAMMY: I said I feel grief, bakkra, not grievance.

PALMER: I know what you said, but I ask you again. You felt grievance against him?

SAMMY: No, bakkra. I know I was wrong to give the niggers salt-beef and salt-pork, and Rhone take my place.

PALMER: What have you done since you put up for sale?

SAMMY: I just sit down in me house.

PALMER: And brood on Rhone.

SAMMY: Brood on the expense I bring down on you. Thirty-five years I serve you and your father, and I never do nutten without yea or nay from the bakkra.

PALMER: You didn't brood on yourself, put up for sale, and on separation from your woman and family.

SAMMY: Well, sir, that is my trial, but I grieve that I took liberties with the trust you put in me, Sammy, and now Rhone is another trial come down on you.

PALMER: Nigger, you playing fool to catch wise.

SAMMY: I stand here under bakkra and God.

PALMER: Who killed Rhone?

SAMMY: Bakkra, I hear about Herrera, but my head refuse. I don't know.

PALMER: Your woman slept in your bed last night?

SAMMY: She was at her usual meeting till cock-crow, bakkra.

PALMER: She made you buy the salt food.

SAMMY: Bakkra, I am in charge of your stores. I was in charge of your stores.

PALMER: Call your wife.

SAMMY: She's waiting bakkra.

PALMER: Call her.

SAMMY: *(Gently.)* Princess. Come Princess.

PRINCESS enters.

PALMER: She made you buy the salt food the day I married?

SAMMY: Bakkra, my wife has enemies in your house. Anything you hear is labrish.

PALMER: I ask you this on oath. Dawes, give him the Bible. Did she make you buy the salt food?

SAMMY: *(Holding the Bible.)* Bakkra, she made me buy the salt food.

PALMER: And you are an honest Christian fool, so you thought your wife was like you, with motives honest and Christian.

SAMMY: She was concerned for the suffering sir.

PALMER: She didn't tell you that the day I married was the day her son was certain not to inherit.

SAMMY: Sir, you gave Cupid his freedom. What more could he want?

PALMER: My five estates. Don't the black people want that? *(Sarcastic.)* Isn't it their land? Isn't your wife in rebellion against me? Doesn't she feed runaways.

SAMMY: I am only her husband sir.

PALMER: And you swear to me now under oath, she is not a rebel.

SAMMY: *(Selling her out.)* I was not at her meeting sir.

PALMER turns to PRINCESS.

PALMER: Where is my wife?

PRINCESS: Hiding from the doctor sir.

PALMER: Princess, somebody give my wife a powder to kill my baby. Who?

PRINCESS: Bakkra, your wife miscarried on the boat.

PALMER: Her nanny was a blasted Ibo slave like you. You gave her powders? You gave my slaves powders.

PRINCESS: Bakkra the women work through sickness till they miscarry. You want more than that? They cook the food they can't eat, wash the clothes they can't wear, and make the beds they can't sleep in. And when they run and you catch them, you cripple them.

PALMER: So you dose-out the baby niggers that I need to grow big and chop cane. And dose-out me son and heir.

PRINCESS: Rebellion is all over the parish and it will be heard right here in your house.

PALMER: Who killed Rhone?

PRINCESS: Well, everybody know how that go.

PALMER: How it go?

PRINCESS: It go beyond mortal control.

PALMER: You grievance Rhone?

PRINCESS: For what sir?

PALMER: Sammy sale.

PRINCESS: Is Rhone sell Sammy, sir?

PALMER: You grievance me?

PRINCESS: I grievance you. Yes bakkra. You sell Sammy.

PALMER: So it's me next?

PRINCESS: Left to me, it's you first, bakkra.

PALMER: So you go to meeting to conspire against me.

PRINCESS: Bakkra the people conspire. And I believe Herrera has some business to settle. With Rhone and Dawes, then with you.

PALMER: Princess, I am a magistrate of this parish. Take the oath.

PRINCESS: No, sir. It's not my God. Leave the book and hang me. When I'm dead and buried I'll rise up and eat food and live and you will die like everything you believe in.

PALMER: Dawes, bear witness. Princess conspire.

PRINCESS: Bakkra, slaves live and die at your pleasure, and I am a slave. But who can chain up the dead? They walk free. Bakkra day done. Black man time come now.

PALMER: You threatenin' my authority?

PRINCESS: Yes.

PALMER: Dawes, take this woman into the slave yard and hang her.

DAWES: Come.

PRINCESS: *(Shouts.)* Tell Cupid to look after all the children.

PALMER: I have changed my mind. Take her to the slave yard, whip her, and then hang her.

All exit, except PALMER and SAMMY.

Sammy. *(He throws him the store keys.)* Count the stores. Top to bottom.

Blackout.

PALMER stands in the drawing-room listening to dogs in the pen howling. SAMMY enters.

PALMER: Where is my wife?

Howling.

SAMMY: Bakkra I know not. The rebellion is spreading. Nine more people run away.

PALMER: *(Bitter comment on SAMMY saying "people", not "niggers".)* They are people now.

SAMMY: Cupid came with rebels and cut Princess down.

PALMER: You counted the stores?

SAMMY: They're half empty.

PALMER: Dawes waits to strike. This mulatto was merely a creature. Black nigger, brown nigger, same nigger. Everywhere you look on the map, black is grief. I'll leave 'em to stink in their bed-sweat, and sell up before the country is weed high. Leave Dawes to me.

A horse pulls up. SAMMY exits. DAWES enters.

SAMMY: You caught her?

DAWES: My men saw her sir.

PALMER: *Your* men, Dawes? You have men?

DAWES: Bakkra is bakkra, and Dawes is his shadow. There is no Dawes without bakkra.

PALMER: Where was she?

DAWES: In the bush, with Cupid.

PALMER: In heat?

DAWES: Yes sir.

PALMER: I want my wife tortured in every particular. Brand her, drag her to the edge of the shit-pit and bury, cut her down with a machete, and bury her. I want this done tonight. *(He gives DAWES the diamond as a reward.)* I'm in your debt.

DAWES: Rape her bakkra?

PALMER: My wife? Are you insane?

ANNIE descends stairs. PALMER exits.

ANNIE: Are you guarding me, Dawes?

DAWES: I fear your husband wants me hanged for your death. I'll bring him home for Christian burial, and woo you with tales of Cupid's demise.

DAWES exits. ANNIE listens to talking-drums in the distance. ABUKU enters, breathless.

ABUKU: Cupid is here!

ANNIE: What are the talking-drums saying Abuku?

ABUKU: Kill the witch.

CUPID enters. Hugs ABUKU and ANNIE.

CUPID: *(To ANNIE.)* Did Dawes tell him?

ANNIE: Yes.

CUPID: Why?

ANNIE: Dawes does the killing and has his own fish to fry.

CUPID: Might you escape?

ANNIE: Yes.

CUPID: The militia hunts me as a rebel, and the rebels fear I'm a traitor.

ANNIE: Did they send you to kill me?

CUPID: Yes.

ANNIE: You know the bush as well as they do. You can hide.

CUPID: We may not meet again. Alive.

ANNIE: Then I'll meet you there.

They look at each other. He runs. ANNIE goes upstairs and lies flat out on her bed.

Lights down. LUCINDA lights candles in the bedroom. DAWES enters drawing-room and goes upstairs to ANNIE, who is still flat out on the bed.

DAWES: *(Frisking her.)* Is milady armed?

ANNIE: Only with my body, Mr. Dawes.

DAWES: You husband's rallying the militia milady, but there are mulattoes among them. Men like me who endured his contempt, and have feelings to vent.

ANNIE: Is he dead?

DAWES: They laced his rum with stagnant water, and he bears a fever.

ANNIE: Will he die?

DAWES: *(Dialect.)* Life gone before doctor come.

ANNIE: Have you forged a new will?

DAWES: When his attorney arrives.

ANNIE: You'll have five estates.

He hangs the diamond PALMER gave him round her neck, parting her cleavage.

ANNIE: I must pillow your bed?

DAWES: Your tits swell for Cupid, and shrivel for me?

ANNIE: You want a quick dip? In his oil? Take those off.

They both undress. He searches the bed, and the pillows, then joins her in the bed.

You need refinements?

DAWES: Yes milady.

ANNIE slips a six inch stiletto from her parts and he gets it in the loins.

Lights up in drawing-room.

ABUKU takes an empty rum-flask from the drawing-room. SAMMY enters.

SAMMY: Milady sent for me?

ABUKU: Yes. *(Very exuberant.)* Mass Sammy, bakkra sent for Princess, and she didn't tremble. Dawes put the rope around her neck, and she wasn't afraid. Niggers know that road well. I will hold their hand and walk it with them.

SAMMY looks distressed. ANNIE enters. ABUKU waits.

ANNIE: Sammy, if anything should happen to Mr. Palmer, will you take charge of the estate?

SAMMY: Yes, milady.

ANNIE: My father cut up some of his land and rented it off. Could that be done here?

SAMMY: And well done, milady, if you find careful tenants.

ANNIE: We must buy our safety. Could all the land on five estates be rented at a pittance, and the tenants freed?

SAMMY: And what would you live on?

ANNIE: We'd grind their cane.

SAMMY: It would shake slavery if the tenants were freed. That's what they fight for. But the estates are Mr. Palmer's and the world hangs on the words of the mighty.

ANNIE: Have you heard from Cupid?

SAMMY: You put Cupid in danger, milady, and you are not safe. You should go back to England.

ANNIE: *(Repeats.)* Have you heard of Cupid.

SAMMY: Cupid is dead.

ANNIE: *(Racing upstairs.)* He is not dead!

SAMMY: The rebels shot him for whitemindedness.

ANNIE: Abuku, come and help me find Cupid.

ANNIE runs into her bedroom to get her shoes and LUCINDA hangs onto them.

LUCINDA: It's not safe out there. If he's alive, he'll come here.

ABUKU: *(To ANNIE.)* Is he alive?

ANNIE: Yes.

LUCINDA: You trust your vision?

ANNIE: Vision comes like a dying ghost.

ABUKU: Will he come?

ANNIE: *(Sobbing.)* He won't leave me, Lucinda, will he?

ABUKU: You put him in danger.

ANNIE: He doesn't care if I'm white, he doesn't think I'm a whore, he knows the politics are deranged, he isn't a blind creature of his time, passing down tried and tested lies.

LUCINDA: Can you *see* Cupid alive?

ANNIE: The rebels didn't kill him. It was the militia that stood him up to be shot for a traitor, the gun flashed in the pan, and he fled.

LUCINDA: You weren't wrong about Herrera.

HERRERA, his body beautifully together, glows in the room. ANNIE spreads a table with a magnificent devil's cloth, like an altar, lit with candles. ABUKU and LUCINDA chant as they all shed their clothes. Talking-drums in the distance.

ANNIE: What are the talking-drums saying?

LUCINDA: Princess, Princess.

ABUKU: They crucify the body.

LUCINDA: And save the christian soul.

ABUKU: They work our bodies to death...

LUCINDA: Making useless silver and sugar and gold.

ABUKU: Our joys are fleeting.

LUCINDA: And our sixth sense is dead.

ANNIE: Oh Satan, fallen angel of joy, fallen angel of love. Restore love to heaven.

LUCINDA: Restore joy to heaven.

ANNIE: God a virgin, Christ a virgin, and virgin the mother of God. Kiss the mountain of shame.

They ritually kiss each others' mons, chanting.

ALL: *(Chanting.)* I see the body of Christ, neither sinful nor crucified.

From the darkness outside comes PALMER's deranged voice, talking to a safe-nigger.

PALMER: I burn a fever. Send in the doctor.

SAFE-NIGGER: He's not here sir.

PALMER: Send him in.

PALMER enters the drawing-room. ABUKU pads in with a flask of rum. PALMER wheels round.

PALMER: *(Screaming.)* Wear shoes!

ABUKU puts the rum on the table.

Where is Dawes?

ABUKU: Dead sir.

PALMER: Milady?

ABUKU: Upstairs sir.

PALMER starts to bolt, hears dogs' feet padding around and dogs growling. He's afraid to go out into the dark. He fires, emptying his gun. ANNIE appears at the top of the stairs.

ANNIE: If you can shoot them, they can't be real.

PALMER: I don't know what is fear and what is real. I know Cupid is gone. He ran out of breath.

ANNIE: Fever won't kill you. You'll blow your brains out and they'll toss you into the shit-pit. That's the way I saw you die the day I married you.

PALMER: Chloe will look after me. *(Shouts.)* Chloe. Chloe!

ANNIE: Chloe's in the slave-gang.

PALMER: My father bought and sold 'em all his life and died laughin' in bed. A tighter fist you never met. Always laughin' and totally joyless. There's peace in England and thrift. We'll heal our quarrel in England…

If you breed.

A son, yes.

ANNIE sees CUPID standing in the door.

ANNIE: *(To PALMER.)* You have a son right here in the house.

PALMER: You had my son! Where is my son?

ANNIE: I pray I am breeding for Cupid, and our love-child shall live.

PALMER, his mind going, hears an imaginary bugle.

PALMER: You hear the bugle. They've caught another rebel. When it blow again they will cut him. The road will be safe, I can go now. I am weak with fever and some fear, and harmless vapours seem real. The world of silver and sugar and gold seems absurd, but it is my world, ruled by a jealous brute with a gun. I'll blow my brains out to prove they're there. I am a scientific man. Don't be alarmed.

He exits. We hear two shots.

SLAVES: *(Off, in the distance.)* Burn the cane, bakkra mad, burn the cane!

ABUKU: *(Entering.)* The army is coming.

CUPID: Where are they?

ABUKU: When they've stopped drinkin' and whorin' they'll come, and we'll piss on their corpses. *(Exit.)*

ANNIE: The murder ends, my lovely Cupid. We're both hanging and swing gently in the wind, out of our foolish bodies, at home in the shades. Go to Africa to see the

God and give him the news, that our best hope was our neighbours got slaughtered, not us.

They look at each other.

End.

EPILOGUE

Meetings with Barry Reckord

The year was 1971. I was in the first term of my first year at drama school. A notice goes up on the information board offering free tickets to students to attend that evening's performance of a new play at the Roundhouse theatre in Chalk Farm. Being new to drama school, new to London, and hungry for experience of theatre I took up the offer. What I saw that evening was a play called *Skyvers*. The play was written by a man called Barry Reckord, and directed by Pam Brighton. I had no idea what to expect when I walked into the theatre. I knew nothing of the writer or director, or the faintest idea what the title might be referring to. Anyway what I got was a riveting indictment of the English education and class system told through the experience of teachers and pupils of a dead-end comprehensive school. The play's theme was education, or more accurately the lack of education and the blighting effect that has. I left the theatre in a state of excitement and shock. Excitement because I'd just watched a dramatization of my feelings. The actors on stage seemed to be feeling the same anger and resentment I was feeling, saying the things I wanted to say, but couldn't. I didn't have the means, and that was shocking, because it meant I had bumped up against someone who I didn't know, never met, but who knew me well enough to explain me on a stage. I suppose it could be said that that was my first encounter with Barry Reckord, and it would be several years before we would actually meet.

Barry Reckord and I met for the first time at the BBC Pebble Mill Television studios in Birmingham. We had gathered to do the 'read through' of Barry's television play, *Club Havana*, part of the second city first series. Everyone who would be involved in the production was present in the room, actors, the director, producers, designers, and some of the film crew, and of course the writer Barry Reckord a little round man in black rimmed glasses, who sat away from everyone in a corner of the room with his head in his hands; a posture he maintained throughout the reading of his play. As we came to the end of the reading his posture changed. He lifted his head; there was a huge grin on his face. He threw his arms wide as if to embrace the whole room, he let out a great gust of laughter, and then said to the whole room 'O God! I'm so happy! You made my play sound the way I wanted it to (pause) that's never happened to me before.' Followed by more laughter from Barry. He seemed to be a man with a huge capacity for joy, which he freely expressed to everyone that came within his orbit.

Over the few weeks we rehearsed and filmed Barry's play I suppose what I saw, and sadly, what I have never seen since, though we both tried, was Barry in harmony, professionally and intellectually within the world he had chosen to express his deeply felt beliefs. His belief as expressed in this piece was that education, a proper education, was the liberating force that freed us from the tyrannies that made us destructive to each other and ourselves. The piece was completed to everyone's satisfaction, and Barry and I embarked on what was for me a remarkable train journey from Birmingham to London, and I believe it was this journey that was the foundation for my friendship with Barry Reckord. As the train sped back to London, back home for both of us, and in my mind that's an important factor, Barry and I began to reveal ourselves to each other, or rather he got me to reveal myself to him. I had never before met someone of his age who showed such fascination in what someone my age might think, and feel, and aspire too. And he did it with such delicacy, enthusiasm, warmth and encouragement that what became clear was his love, and interest in the young. What he also did on that journey was exchange my thoughts, feelings, for his experience, and how his experience had brought him to where he was at this moment as we headed for home. There seemed to be key incidents in his life, that he carried with him, and had honed down to its essences, so as to demonstrate how unnecessarily brutish life could be. He believed there was another way, which he subtly tried to give you a glimpse of, for you to take or leave as you saw fit. He did this with such zest and good humour, that it became apparent what a brilliant teacher he might have been, and I was glad that I had the good fortune to spend that time with him.

Our meetings by necessity or design became less frequent, but for me always memorable. They would go something like this; out of the blue I would get a phone call from Barry demanding that I come for lunch, because, and I quote, 'I am simply longing to see you.' I duly obliged when I could. Who could refuse such a gracious offer? The lunch in the beginning was always at his home, a flat he shared with the indomitable Diana Athill; whenever I suggested that we might go out to lunch, his riposte was why spend money on something he could do perfectly well, and he could and did – Barry was a generous host. There was always plenty of meat. Barry loved his meat. We would eat, sometimes with Diana, sometimes not, then he would light his pipe, pour himself a whiskey, stretch out on a comfortable surface like a well-fed cat, and so begin his inquiry. How was I? How was the world treating me, and so on? He was always eager to hear how other people were getting on in the world; whether battles were being won or lost. For him that was no longer the question. He had made up his mind about what was important, and if the world disagreed then so be it, there would be no compromise, and he lived accordingly. He wrote what he wanted to in the full knowledge that it would more than likely be rejected, but somehow that never dimmed his enthusiasm; he was never bitter or pessimistic, and when occasionally he showed me what he'd been writing I would see what brilliant perceptions he was capable of, but if that meant straying from his preoccupations he simply lost interest. That is the man, and I admire and respect him for it.

The most surprising meeting I had with Barry was in Weston-Super-Mare. Surprising because Weston as it's known to the locals is a rather sleepy typical English seaside town full of retired gentle folk pottering around waiting to die, and the last place on earth I expected to run into Barry Reckord. I was there on tour with a play called *Driving Miss Daisy* playing the part of the chauffeur, whose raison d'être was to make sure his employer, a cantankerous elderly white woman got to where ever she needed to be safely. For those who don't know, the play is set in America's Deep South, over a twenty-year period before and during the civil rights struggle. The sort of play I imagined Barry would hate, but he didn't. He found it utterly fascinating in the same way an entomologist, having stumbled on a hitherto undiscovered species of bug might. His analysis of the play made me laugh for a long time.

Another meeting with Barry Reckord that stays in the mind was running into him on Primrose Hill in the Regent's Park area of London. We were headed in opposite directions, but collided on the brow of the hill. After a few moments contemplating the marvellous view of London that was afforded from where we stood, Barry began his forensic enquiry into just how was I doing personally, and then the question he left till last: did I have work and what was it? I told him yes I did have work, and at the moment I was playing Macbeth in *Macbeth*. Barely pausing for breath Barry retorted, it's a rotten plot, Shakespeare couldn't really do plots. I said, but the words are good! Barry's response was, 'sometimes, but not as good as Keats.' As if to prove his point he recited some Keats for me. Beautiful, but to my mind inconclusive. We agreed to disagree, and headed off in our different directions. As I walked away from Barry I realized what it was I loved about him, and would always treasure. Put simply – it was his irreverence. Nothing was beyond question, everything, whatever it was, for its own sake, and ours, needed to be tested from time to time. Barry lived his life in that fashion. He is entirely *sui generis*. Much Love, Don.

Don Warrington

Barry Reckord: Biography

Barry Reckord was born in Jamaica on 19th November 1926, and went to Britain in the 1950s to study at Cambridge University as an Issa scholar. His first play *Della* (1953) under the title *Flesh to a Tiger* was produced at the Royal Court in 1958. He wrote several more plays for the Royal Court in the late 1950s and early 1960s including *You In Your Small Corner* (1961), *Skyvers* (1963,1971) and *X* (1974). In 1962 Reckord adapted *You in Your Small Corner* for the Independent Television *Play of The Week* series. He wrote two more television dramas for the BBC: *In The Beautiful Caribbean* broadcast on the 3rd February 1972 and *Club Havana* transmitted on the 25th October 1975. In 1973 he was awarded a Jamaican Silver Musgrave Medal for his contribution to playwriting and was made a Fellow of the Guggenheim Memorial Foundation in the same year. His treatise on Cuba and its Revolution, *Does Fidel Eat More Than Your Father? Cuban Opinion* was published in 1971 (London: Deutsch; New York: Prager).

List of works:

Theatre

1953	*Della*	Ward Theatre, Kingston, Jamaica
1954	*Adella*	London fringe
1956	*Miss Unusual*	Jamaica
1958	*Flesh to a Tiger (Della)*	Royal Court Theatre, London
1960	*You in Your Small Corner*	Cheltenham
1961	*You in Your Small Corner*	Royal Court Theatre, London
		Arts Theatre, London
1962	*You in Your Small Corner*	Ward Theatre, Kingston, Jamaica
1963	*Skyvers*	Royal Court Theatre, London
1963	*I Man* (title of *Skyvers* in Jamaica)	Jamaica
1968	*Skyvers*	Nottingham Playhouse
1968	*You in Your Small Corner*	Arts Lecture Theatre, UWI, Kingston Jamaica
1969	*Don't Gas the Blacks*	Open Space Theatre, London
1970	*A Liberated Woman*	New Arts Lecture Theatre at the UWI Kingston, Jamaica November 28
1970	*June Fishing*	Jamaica
1971	*A Liberated Woman*	Royal Court Theatre, London
1971	*A Liberated Woman*	La Mama, New York, March 17
1971	*Skyvers* (revival)	Royal Court Theatre Upstairs
1971	*Skyvers*	Roundhouse, London
1972	*In the Beautiful Caribbean*	Ward Theatre Kingston, Jamaica. April 22nd
1973	*Let it All Hang Out, Daddy*	Lecture Theatre, University of the West Indies Kingston, Jamaica, December

1973	*Give the Gaffers Time to Love You*	Sunday reading, Royal Court Theatre, May 18
1974	*X (Let It All Hang Out Daddy)*	Theatre Upstairs, Royal Court Theatre, London
1975	*The White Witch of Rose Hall*	Creative Arts Centre, Kingston, Jamaica, October
1978	*The White Witch of Rose Hall*	Creative Arts Centre, Kingston, Jamaica
1979	*The Family Bed* (reworking of *X*)	unproduced
1980	*Joshua versus Spiderman*[1]	Jamaica
1981	*Skyvers* amateur production	London (YAT)
1982	*Streetwise* (musical adaptation of *Skyvers*)	London/Bristol
1985	*White Witch*	Rehearsed reading, Tricycle Theatre, London
1988	*Let It All Hang Out Daddy* (or *X*)	Kingston
1988	*Sugar D*	Barn Theatre, Kingston
2006	*Skyvers* (50 rehearsed readings series)	Royal Court January 23rd

Adaptations

1989	*Beverly Hills Call Girl* (from both the *Ladies and Gentlemen* & *The Balloons in the Black Bag* by William Donaldson) – produced and directed by Barry Reckord. July 21. New Kingston Theatre.

Plays for Television

TV Play of the Week	Granada	*You in Your Small Corner* (1962) single TV drama
Play for Today	BBC	*In the Beautiful Caribbean* (1972) single TV drama
Second City Firsts	BBC	*Club Havana* (1975) single TV drama

---

1   Reworking of *In the Beautiful Caribbean*. Also known as *...Michael*

Notes on Contributors

DIANA ATHILL was born in Norfolk in 1917 and educated at home until she was fourteen. She read English at Lady Margaret Hall, Oxford and graduated in 1939. She spent the war years working at the BBC Overseas Service in the News Information Department. After the war she met Andre Deutsch and fell into publishing. She worked as an editor, first at Allan Wingate and then at Andre Deutsch, until her retirement at the age of 75 in 1993. Her books include *An Unavoidable Delay, After a Funeral, Make Believe, Instead of a Letter, Don't Look at Me Like That, Stet* (her memoir of fifty years in publishing) and most recently *Somewhere Towards the End*, winner of the 2008 Costa Prize for Biography.

PAM BRIGHTON began working as an assistant director at the Royal Court in London. She then worked at many theatres in England. She was Artistic Director of the Half Moon, Hull Truck and Double Joint. She lived and worked in Canada for four years. She is well known for her style of popular political theatre, as in *Skyvers, The Housing Show, George Davis is Innocent OK, Binlids* and *The Laughter of Our Children*.

YVONNE BREWSTER, founder member of the Barn Theatre (Jamaica) and Talawa Theatre Company (UK) has worked in theatre, film, television, radio, and universities as a director, lecturer and actor. She is a Fellow of Rose Bruford College, Central School of Speech and Drama and the Royal Society of Arts, a Licentiate of the Royal College of Music. She received the OBE for Services to the Arts (1993) and an Honorary Doctorate from the Open University (2001). She edited three collections in the Methuen series *Black Plays*. Her autobiography *The Undertaker's Daughter* was published in 2004.

MERVYN MORRIS, Professor Emeritus of Creative Writing and West Indian Literature at the University of the West Indies, is the author of *Is English We Speaking: And Other Essays* (Ian Randle Publishers, 1999), *Making West Indian Literature* (IRP, 2005) and six books of poetry, including *I Been There, Sort Of: New and Selected Poems* (Carcanet Press, 2006). He has been a theatre reviewer for *The Daily Gleaner*, *The Sunday Sun* and *The Jamaica Observer*.

DON WARRINGTON, renowned Black British actor, emigrated to Newcastle, England from Trinidad in 1961. Perhaps best known for his portrayal of Philip Smith in the sitcom *Rising Damp*, his career has included many other leading TV roles including Nigel Beaumont in *C.A.T.S. Eyes*, Judge Ken Winyard in *New Street Law* and Patrick in *Manchild*. In theatre, Clifton in *Elmina's Kitchen* and Kwaku in *Statement of Regret* at the National Theatre are his most recent portrayals. In 2008 he attained 'celebrity' status when he became a contestant in *Strictly Come Dancing* on BBC Television. Mr. Warrington was awarded an MBE in 2008 for his services to drama and serves on the Board of Talawa Theatre Company.

Acknowledgements

I am most grateful for the support of members of Barry Reckord's family: Lloyd Reckord, his brother, founding Artistic Director of the Jamaica National Theatre Trust, who loaned me programmes of his company's productions of *In The Beautiful Caribbean*, *The White Witch* 1975 and *The White Witch* 1978 from his archive. Michael Reckord for making available his interview with Barry Reckord published in *The Gleaner* in 2003, Margaret Bernal for the loan of newspaper clippings of reviews of *Skyvers* 1971 and for making a chronological listing of Barry Reckord's works as found in *The Jamaica National Theatre Trust: a Local Theatre with a World View* by Cynthia Reckord (1983 thesis, UWI, re-edited by Margaret Reckord Bernal [2008]) available to me. I thank them all for their unstinting assistance and encouragement. Without access to the archives of Jamaica National Theatre Trust, under whose auspices much of Barry's work in Jamaica was produced, my job would have been well nigh impossible. Through the kindness of Dr. Beverly Hart of the Victoria and Albert Museum archives the prompt copy of the Royal Court production of *Flesh To A Tiger* in 1958 was searched for and found. I am indebted to her for her help. Deep gratitude is due to Diana Athill who at the age of 92 sat on the floor pulling out stacks of odd pages of manuscripts much dog eared and in some chaos to help with the search for the texts, and to Munair Zacca and Errol Lloyd who searched and found original copies of *The White Witch* 1978, 1985. To Professor Mervyn Morris, Don Warrington, Joan Ann Maynard, Michael Abbensetts, Errol Lloyd, Sebastian Born, Professor Barry Chevannes, Carrol Chin Lenn, Andrew Walby, Starr Brewster, Roland Rees and last but certainly not least Pam Brighton, much appreciation is due.

Yvonne Brewster